Slow Adventism

Slow Adventism

Ecclesiological Holzwege

HANZ GUTIERREZ SALAZAR

*Forewords by
Abigail Doukhan
and Zane Yi*

WIPF & STOCK · Eugene, Oregon

SLOW ADVENTISM
Ecclesiological Holzwege

Copyright © 2025 Hanz Gutierrez Salazar. All rights reserved. Except for brief quotations in critical publications or reviews, no part of this book may be reproduced in any manner without prior written permission from the publisher. Write: Permissions, Wipf and Stock Publishers, 199 W. 8th Ave., Suite 3, Eugene, OR 97401.

Wipf & Stock
An Imprint of Wipf and Stock Publishers
199 W. 8th Ave., Suite 3
Eugene, OR 97401

www.wipfandstock.com

PAPERBACK ISBN: 979-8-3852-6348-6
HARDCOVER ISBN: 979-8-3852-6349-3
EBOOK ISBN: 979-8-3852-6350-9

VERSION NUMBER 11/20/25

Scripture quotations are taken from the Holy Bible, New International Version®, NIV® Copyright © 1973, 1978, 1984, 2011 by Biblica, Inc. Used with permission. All rights reserved worldwide.

To the GC President, Erton Köhler,
who, like me, belongs to the noble
and wise South-American Adventist diaspora—
Capable of understanding that mission is not refined proselytism,
that South American Adventism is not all Adventism,
that Adventism is not all Christianity,
and that Christianity is not all humanity.

To Daniel, Bryan, Linda, Melody,
And to Winnie, Schak, Cody, Icy
For having made my life slower and fuller

Contents

Foreword by Abigail Doukhan | ix
Foreword by Zane Yi | xiii
Introduction | xvii

Part I: Compulsions and Sublimations
1 Oppression, Performativity, and Weariness of the Self | 3
2 Adventism and the Challenge of Inculturation | 31
3 The Elusiveness of the Particular: On Micro-Stories | 36
4 Complexity and Diasporic Identities | 43
5 The Ambivalence of Militancy | 48
6 The Challenge of Bottom-Up Ethics | 53
7 Against Rectitude | 59
8 The Trap of Theological Universalism | 65

Part II: Vulnerability and Flourishing
9 A Reasonable Adventism | 73
10 The Need for a Slow Church | 81
11 Centripetal and Centrifugal Adventism | 88
12 A Post-Whitean Adventism | 94
13 A Post-Apocalyptic Adventism | 100
14 Praise of Laodicea | 106
15 The Value of a Kenotic Adventism | 111
16 Rootedness, Inclusiveness, and Flourishing | 117

Contents

Conclusion | 163
Bibliography | 165
Author Index | 175

Foreword
by Abigail Doukhan

THIS BOOK IS A rescue mission! It is a courageous and passionate attempt to break Adventism out of an outdated eigtheenth-century conceptual prison that has been increasingly limiting and impeding its original impulse. It is a delicate endeavor to untangle Adventism from the rigid, authoritarian, and solipsistic framework of modernity in a desperate attempt to crack open a different path—a new path—a path willing to break old molds and move into new spaces that are open and respectful of otherness as well as sensitive/permeable to the self's emotional life, to the rages, passions and questions that foment beneath the surface of our polished and pious selves. At its heart, this book is the uncovering of a lost and forgotten forest path, a *Holzwege* that allows us to meander, to venture beyond the familiar, even to lose our way and to take things slowly. Indeed, what Gutierrez criticizes is not so much Adventism—itself originally a movement in constant evolution—but what Adventism, under the influence of modernity, has become.

But what is modernity? Modernity is a euro-centric philosophical framework that arose in the eighteenth century during the Enlightenment that sought to articulate once and for all what it meant to be human, with categories that were built to mold our societal differences and the complex emotions pulsating through our humanity, for the sake of a rational, ordered, and shared universal definition of the self. The emphasis was what we had in common, and the desire was to crystallize us around these commonalities in order to forge a peaceful and harmonious society. The problem with this framework, however, consisted in the ejection of all that separated us, that distinguished us: our particularities, our contradictions, our complexity. It was also the repression of anything that might disturb the precarious mastery and ordered world of the rational self—our emotions, our rages, our despairs, our passions, and our darker pulsions.

Gutierrez argues that Adventism, unbeknownst to itself, and in contradistinction with its original impulse to be a movement open to ever new blessings, revelations, and orientations, has little by little adopted the modern framework of seeking to rally its members around a rigid and fixed concept of "truth," leaving little room for dissent, conflict, and further exploration. And that, pedagogically speaking, in the inculcating of these "truths," Adventism has failed to honor a space for the self's emotional and critical response to its teachings. The result has been a deepening neglect of complex emotions, dissent, and doubt—in a word, a denial of our humanity. More treacherously, this rallying of our movement around universal "truths" has left no room for other ways of thinking, feeling, and doing, thereby systematically threatening the dimension of otherness in our midst.

In this critique of this modernist version of Adventism, Gutierrez follows the trajectory of critical thinkers born out of the postmodern backlash to modernity, allowing for their critique to illuminate what, in our faith, has become outdated, suffocating, and rigid. The book is divided into two sections: one critical of outdated frameworks in which Adventism has become trapped, and one offering new visions for our movement. In the first part of the book, each chapter of the book explores one aspect of our faith that has become trapped in the straightjacket of modernity in the light of the critical reflections of thinkers such as Heidegger, Simmel, Kundera, and Ginzburg. As such, Gutierrez is not so much doing systematic philosophy (creating a system of thought for our church) as un-systematic philosophy, i.e., deconstructing the system in which our faith has become trapped in order to liberate it, oxygenate it, and let it catch its original "breath," the breath of the Spirit that first animated it, thereby attempting to give Adventism a renewed impulse and relevance. Such is the gesture performed in the second part of the book, where new orientations for our faith are proposed.

But more than dissecting Adventism with the scalpel of postmodern thought and opening up new horizons and orientations for it, I believe Gutierrez is uncovering a more ancient path, or *Holzwege*—a path that the biblical text itself invites us to walk in—the path of iconoclasm, of exile, of the *lech lecha*, and of openness to the other. This is the path of Abraham, the first believer, the first friend of God, the path that leads away from rigid systems of thought—the very definition of idolatry—into ever new territories, still to come, still to be revealed, still to be discovered. This is the path explored by the wisdom literature corpus within the biblical text itself, where potentially rigid institutions, ethnocentric and oppressive structures, are deconstructed and critiqued by the biblical writers themselves, allowing for new spaces to be opened: spaces welcoming of otherness, of complexity, of dissent, and of uncharted exploration. Such are the books of Job, of Ruth, and of Ecclesiastes. Finally, this is the path that Jesus himself charted when he spoke of acquiring new wineskins capable of holding the fresh wine of novel revelations, new impulses, and new life.

It is this ongoing openness to new truths and new epiphanies that Gutierrez means when he speaks of "kenotic" Adventism. For too long, Adventism has allowed itself to be ossified into the framework of modernity. This book explodes these outdated categories and invites us to journey anew, to explore anew, and to take the risk of genuine connection—with both our intimate selves and with others—which characterizes the authentic quest for truth. As Martin Buber says so beautifully, God is not in another galaxy sitting on a lofty and authoritarian throne but "between us." He dwells in all genuine conversations with one's spirit and with others, and in our capacity to remain open, sensitive, and, especially, human.

Abigail Doukhan
Queens College–Philosophy
The City University of New York
New York, USA

Foreword
by Zane Yi

Holzwege is the German word for "forest path," an analogy in philosophy for thinking differently through the tangle of something familiar. The subtitle of this work reminds me of the opening lines of a celebrated poem.

"Two roads diverged in a yellow wood," writes Robert Frost in "The Road Not Taken." The traveler cannot walk them both, so he stands indecisively at the crossroad. Which should he take—the one that looks well-worn and weathered by frequent use, or the other, overgrown and wild?

In reading the pages you now hold, I recalled the first time I met Hanz Gutierrez over fifteen years ago. As Adventists who had acquired formal training in "the love of wisdom," we were fellow travelers on a road less traveled. Our paths converged in Atlanta, Georgia, for the inaugural gathering of The Society of Adventist Philosophers. Dr. Gutierrez, or "Hanz," as we eventually fondly grew to address him, had flown in from Italy to present a paper.

As a graduate student, I remember being struck by both what Hanz had to say and how he said it, even if I can't remember the details of his paper all these years later. What he had to share was informed by a deep study of philosophy as well as an international perspective.

He thought and talked carefully and deeply . . . slowly.

I was also impressed to learn that he was a physician as well as a professor of theology.

My early memories of Hanz, and what I have grown to know and appreciate about his years of faithful ministry and courageous scholarship, converge in this latest book. In it, he yields the scalpel of philosophical analysis to diagnose a long-term patient—his beloved Seventh-day Adventist community—who does not seem to realize they are sick.

We, those who belong to this community, have collectively wandered down the wrong path and Gutierrez calls us back, imploring us to consider an alternative one—the *holzwege*—one that leads to a healthier future.

The problem, as Gutierrez sees it, continues to be his patient's uncritical acceptance of the tenets of modernity. The analysis he offers is similar to—in many ways, a continuation of—the one he makes in his previous work *Beyond the Bible, Beyond the West*. In this work, the focus is on the interpretation of the Bible, which Gutierrez insightfully points out has been interpreted through the methods and standards of Enlightenment rationalism. Texts are treated reductively, as readers look for a single, timeless meaning.

Hanz challenges us to think about Scripture differently, as containing more and many meanings that exceed narrow and shallow anticipations.

In this most recent work, Hanz's focus shifts to addressing the way we think about Christian community—"ecclesiology." Here again, his patient has innocently ingested a toxic concoction of modernistic values and norms. This time, the source is Enlightenment political philosophy and economic theory that values uniformity, efficiency, and productivity.

The church unwittingly organizes itself like a multinational business corporation, seeking rapid growth for the sake of growth.

But this, as has been pointed out by others, is "the ideology of cancer cells."

Is bigger always better?

Does faster lead to flourishing?

Hanz encourages us to reconsider these fundamental questions, answering them in the negative. We should not confuse the metrics of the Spirit with those of the quarterly earnings report provided to please shareholders.

He invites us to consider the alternative of a slower Adventism, one more rooted in particular times and places of the many local communities that collectively comprise the sisterhood of the Adventist churches.

One size, here, does not fit all.

If so, what might bind this diverse community together? Again, Hanz argues that we need more options than the binary ones provided to us by modern philosophy: either correct common beliefs or correct practices, i.e., orthodoxy or orthopraxy.

What holds the church together is "orthopathy," or right emotion, i.e., compassion, as Jesus so clearly taught.

Foreword

Or in the words of a familiar song, "They will know that we are Christians by our love."

The emphasis on the other options, as Hanz points out, is overly intellectual or pragmatic, again—unbeknownst to many—mirroring the ideals of Enlightenment philosophy.

I'm grateful to Hanz for the gift of this book, one that inspires and challenges us to think differently about what it means to be a global community of congregations and individuals, rooted in various places, seeking life for all. May it be widely discussed, debated, and lived in diverse contexts.

Like the intrepid traveler in Frost's poem, perhaps we need to return to consider and walk the road "less traveled by." And, similarly, perhaps this will make "all the difference" in our life together, as well as on behalf of others.

Zane Yi
School of Religion
Loma Linda University
California, USA

Introduction

"Slow Adventism" sounds like a downward compromise, a sort of submissive, accommodating, and resigned Adventism, of which nobody would like to be a part. On the contrary, we would all like a dynamic, proactive, culturally relevant church, able to immediately get in touch with the big transformations of our time and rapidly propose true alternatives. But, as often happens, it's not easy to know the nature of our historical time and in which way and proportion churches are real alternatives or just sophisticated extensions of the cultural season they want to correct. Theoretically, churches tend to resist or even contradict their own cultural context in order to create a reasonable justification for their own mission. But it's not guaranteed that opposition or even contradiction by itself creates true alternatives. Very often, opposing movements share common cultural presuppositions and perspectives. That seems to be the case in today's Adventism. The typical future-oriented, pragmatic, dynamic, rational, efficient, coherent, and creative spirit of modern societies seems to be assumed passively by Adventism, even if it's grounded differently—not on reason or science but in God's will and on the Bible. As a result, the final picture gives a sort of hidden twinning between the "performative, precise, and accelerated society" we belong to and a "performative, precise, and accelerated Adventism" that, in secondary dimensions, keeps criticizing and fighting each other in order to maintain and value what they believe to be the specifics and particularities of their own mission.

A "fast Adventism," as much as a hypertrophic body, nevertheless, is not necessarily more performant. "Faster" and "bigger" are not necessarily synonyms of health or flourishing. In order for somebody or something to flourish, it may be necessary to recover incompleteness, vulnerability, and

Introduction

slowness as necessary and primordial conditions in becoming human, as Spanish philosopher Josep Maria Esquirol reminds us in his beautiful book *Humà, més humà*.[1] Full and plethoric entities are inappropriate and unprepared to flourish because they are not touched by a beneficial emptiness that is essential for surviving and entering into relationship. As much as persuasive and touching melodies presuppose and include silence and pauses, so healthy beings are not plethoric but intermittent and interrupted entities; they are "reasonable beings" who have learned to perceive life's systole and diastole as mechanisms that support life in its contractions and expansions, in its affirmation and flexibility, in its giving and receiving in the context of the multiple relationships that life offers and demands from us.

Fourteen of the sixteen chapters in this book have appeared previously in *Spectrum* online magazine in a series titled "Ecclesiological Holzwege." The two traits present in the subtitle are not circumstantial but are already part of my way of doing theology. First, *Holzwege*, which means partial, interrupted, overlapping, plural, and provisional paths in a forest, because theology has been and will always be dialogical and experimental. Of this fact, "spectrum" is a clear sign and witness for already various decades in and outside Adventism. Second, "Ecclesiological" because throughout the book is disseminated a constant critique of the concept of anthropological sovereignty based on autonomy, will, and reason. The implicit and explicit critique and correction of this drift is the bet on relationship and bonding. I take "ecclesiological," in this positive sense, as a mode of privileging relations over social and religious atomization.

The first and last chapters are biblical–cultural reflections on Ps 137 and Ps 1 with intent to delineate, in dialogue with the Bible, our present sociocultural context, without which it is impossible to do any type of constructive theology. For the same contextual reason, European Adventism (Italy), is the main perspective—presupposed and imagined, premise and claim, description and dream—which twirls and meanders through each of these sixteen meditations.

A particular and deep felt thanks to Steve Chavez, Kärt Lazic and Alexander Carpenter (Spectrum), for having read the manuscript and for their precious suggestions.

This book on Ecclesiology is part of a larger project that will be published in the coming years following this general structure:

---

1. Esquirol, *Humà, més humà*.

Introduction

1. God: He Who Doesn't Know—*Theological Holzwege*
2. Eu-topia: Sabbath, Embodiment, and Emplacement—*Cosmological Holzwege*
3. Emmanu-ology: Valorization and Transformation—*Soteriological Holzwege*
4. Slow Adventism: *Ecclesiological Holzwege*
5. Flourishing, Desire, and Joy: *Ethical Holzwege*
6. Eu-schatology: Vulnerability, Hopelessness, and Trust—*Messianic Holzwege*

PART I

Compulsions and Sublimations

1

Oppression, Performativity, and Weariness of the Self

For there our captors asked us for songs, our tormentors demanded songs of joy.

PSALM 137:3

PSALM 137

I

[1] By the rivers of Babylon we sat and wept
when we remembered Zion.
[2] There on the poplars
we hung our harps,
[3] for there our captors asked us for songs,
our tormentors demanded songs of joy;
they said, "Sing us one of the songs of Zion!"

II

[4] How can we sing the songs of the Lord
while in a foreign land?
[5] If I forget you, Jerusalem,
may my right hand forget its skill.

> ⁶ May my tongue cling to the roof of my mouth
>   if I do not remember you,
> if I do not consider Jerusalem
>   my highest joy.
>
> **III**
> ⁷ Remember, Lord, what the Edomites did
>   on the day Jerusalem fell.
> "Tear it down," they cried
>   "tear it down to its foundations!"
> ⁸ Daughter Babylon, doomed to destruction,
>   happy is the one who repays you
>   according to what you have done to us.
> ⁹ Happy is the one who seizes your infants
>   and dashes them against the rocks.

THIS PSALM, IN HERMANN Gunkel's classification, is a mixed poem containing a communal lament along with a hymn of gratitude and thankfulness.[1] The Psalm is divided into three stanzas.[2] The first stanza describes the exile experience in Babylon and the unbearable burden of longing for the land of Israel. The second stanza describes the tension of wanting to praise, but at the same time not doing so because they are far from their land. The third, on the other hand, describes the oppressed paradoxical demand for revenge with respect to Edom and Babylon for what they have done to Israel.

I. LINGUISTIC OPPRESSION: LAMENTATION AS RESISTANCE

Oppression does not necessarily begin with an overbearing physical act but rather with a dissimulating and stigmatizing language of the people we want to oppress and, at the same time, with a legitimizing language of abusive power. Antonio Gramsci recalled this from prison, thus drawing attention to the need for a linguistic-cultural uprising before a military revolution that aims to overthrow that which he called the oppressive "superstructure" (culture, ideas, language), more hidden and more elusive

---

1. Gunkel, *Einleitung in die Psalmen*.
2. Ravasi, *Salmi*, 566–69; Lancellotti, *Salmi*, 875–79; Mays, *Psalms*, 421–24; Brueggemann, *Psalms*, 572–76.

than that economic "structure," which instead appears as a more explicit and visible dimension of an oppressive system.[3]

Psalm 137 offers the possibility of grasping these various registers of oppression, including the linguistic dimension, and helps us think about oppression in its most paradoxical and hidden forms.

Together with the description of a problem, the psalm adds a prescription that aims to offer a way out, but which is not articulated directly. The description of a problem would not necessarily diminish the suffering that derives from it, but would risk, on the contrary, increasing it if it is not combined with a proposed solution. In fact, the psalm, which is essentially a descriptive exercise, nevertheless elaborates an indirect prescription in that it suggests alternatives of resistance through reflection. The psalm itself is a linguistic form of resistance configured as a "lament."

J. L. Austin, in his book *How to Do Things with Words*, has drawn our attention to a dimension of language that, until then, had been neglected and obscured by the typical and primordial "communicative" dimension of language.[4] The "performative" dimension of language, Austin recalled, is just as important as the communicative one precisely because, without it, language would easily become an ethereal illusion and a sublimatory and refined validation of the status quo.[5]

The performative dimension of language, reminds Austin, allows us to do things with words. This performative aspect of language has allowed oppressors to oppress their victims before using physical force by using alienating, stigmatizing, and deforming words. The first form of linguistic oppression is to cancel words and categories that express pain, suffering, and frustration. For this reason, the first step to freedom is not physical but linguistic, in finding words of liberation. The first linguistic register in order to resist oppression and to trigger liberation, from the Ps 137 perspective, is "lamentation." Through lamentation, we give voice to pain, frustration, and oppression. By doing so, we resist and build up liberation. Lamentation is a prayer that, in Ps 137 and in the Psalms in general, embodies three important dimensions of the faith experience.

---

3. Gramsci, *Quaderni del carcere*, 5–13.
4. Austin, *How to Do Things*, 11–22.
5. Austin, *How to Do Things*, 11–22.

Part I: Compulsions and Sublimations

a. Psychological Inclusion

The first is a psychological dimension. Believers are granted the right to feel bad, uncertain, or fearful, and to express this discomfort without suffering scorn and condemnation from others. Part of biblical anthropology, especially in the psalms, is the recognition of a structural vulnerability of human beings and a parallel literary form available to give expression to that vulnerability as being a legitimate part of our humanity. Vulnerability does not always provide an adequate and proportional reaction or response. With vulnerability, purely suffered and unacknowledged, often comes fear and blockage, but also the opposite: aggression and violence. This is why one of the first emotional tasks is to look vulnerability in the eye as a fellow traveler and, by trying to understand and accept it, allow it to make us more human and empathetic. Vulnerability, through lamentation, becomes an ally instead of an enemy—a space of self-knowledge and a space for an appropriate understanding of the world and reality. It helps us grasp and comprehend better that we are not self-sufficient. It is precisely by virtue of and through this incompleteness that the desire to be related to others in a timely manner arises in us.

b. Linguistic Inclusion

The second important dimension of lamentation as a form of prayer is linguistic. What would we do with pain and suffering if we lack a suitable language to express them? Very little would remain after the emotional outburst of the initial moment. Pain would struggle to express itself because it would perceive the foreignness of its being to the current and common language. We are not speaking here of a rational need to understand pain as much as of the possibility of expressing it even without understanding it. Pain can and should be expressed and recognized as belonging to us before (and even without taking advantage of any) rational comprehension. Pain is not human only when we understand it; it belongs to us and is ours even when it remains beyond our ideological explanations. There is undoubtedly a more rational register to try to understand and explain it. But for most, pain is beyond any possible rational equation. It is ineffable, inexpressible in words, and incomprehensible with ideas. The fact of not understanding it doesn't mean that it ceases to be part of our innermost history. For this reason, pre-modern cultures, including Old and New Testament cultures, beyond their limitations, could offer and even boast of having linguistic registers and literary forms created specifically to facilitate the expression of pain and thus try to mitigate it. Lamentation as a literary form designed for this purpose. Our contemporary culture, which includes churches and religious communities, is the expression of a cultural regression and involution through the erasure, at least partially, of linguistic registers to express pain. Grief and the ability to grieve reminds us of Judith Butler, who maintains that, on average, pain unacknowledged or restricted produces disembodied individuals who don't possess the essential psychological tools to express themselves linguistically and socially.[6]

c. Cultural Inclusion

The third dimension of lamentation fulfills a sociocultural function—that of slowing down the pace of human activities. Pre-modern societies were slow for this reason; they perceived, dialogued with, and respected pain by giving it time and space. Pain slows down life's rhythm. In this context, excessive conformity and passivity in front of it can certainly emerge with the intent of taking it seriously. But, as in any event, we cannot judge a cultural or religious orientation as wrong just by assessing its extremes and radicalized forms. Accepting pain instead of fighting it often took the extreme form of surrendering and capitulation. Behind this surrendering, however, we must value the intention of searching for a necessary compromise in the face of an event bigger than us. We must understand and try to confront pain wherever and whenever it arise. Pain cannot be prevented and programmed; it is a cultural virtue and must be listed as an asset, even though it breaks the regularity of life's schemes and strategies. Programming pain, on the other hand, beyond the right and necessary minimal arrangements to manage it, is in fact a way of denying it. No pain is regular, proportional, conventional, and foreseeable. Pain always brings a surplus of challenge and discomfort, and this fact will always unsettle us.

Ours have become, for all intents and purposes, "algo-phobic"[7] societies and churches, not because pain is necessarily denied but mainly because we try to program it according to our spatial and temporal patterns that

---

6. Butler, "Grievability for the Living," 89–99.

7. "Algo-phobic" is the attitude that avoids, overlooks, hides, and negates pain because one is fearful and anguished with the idea of having to face it.

are oriented to efficiency.[8] To guarantee efficiency, the space and time offered to perceive pain must necessarily be shortened and limited, otherwise production would be compromised. For this reason, we struggle not only to understand pain but also the abandonment that is intimately linked to pain. As humans, as in any other historical period, we all experience the feeling of being left behind. Abandonment today is experienced as loneliness. Between "abandonment" and "loneliness," the common element is that of detachment. At some point, we feel detached, cut off from the whole that should serve as a womb and container. But the mechanism behind them is different.

In "loneliness," a typical individualist form of abandonment, one loses the sense of primary belonging and consequently feels lonely from the first moment of existence. Before everything and before any event, I am alone— alone with myself and my conscience—ready to choose my own allegiances and interests that I have. Modern individualism is both strong and weak, courageous and hypochondriac, creative and depressed, transgressive and conformist. As a free individual, no one else is with me. I alone, by choice, bind myself to others transiently and through a contract with an expiration date. The chosen bond is certainly clearer and smarter but not necessarily better. In fact, chosen bonds tend to be intense but short. They are weak and transitory precisely because they are chosen and intentional. A chosen bond, because it's based on circumstantial and limited information and awareness, depends only on the individual. For this reason, it is intermittent, short-term, and doesn't benefit from the unconditional and permanent bond offered by groups.

In "abandonment," on the other hand, a pre-modern form of feeling detached from others, which is present in this psalm, may be opaque, partially absent, but nevertheless always there. Its presence is always presupposed and is not the result of a choice but more informed on the basis of personal and ethical awareness. In this perspective, abandonment presupposes a strong type of bonding that is no longer present in modern loneliness. This is why the lamentation of the abandoned has an interlocutor, whereas in modern individualistic lamentation, the interlocutor tends not to be there or to be there in a purely circumstantial and contractual way.

---

8. This is the term used by Byung-Chul Han to refer to societies, such as ours, that tend to banish suffering and pain from daily life. Of course, no one can completely erase pain, but algo-phobic societies tend to cushion its impact through certain mechanisms such as sedation or concentration of pain only at certain times. See Han, *Società senza dolore*, 5–12.

There is no certainty of being heard by anyone else but us. We have doubted the world (Descartes), then the world evaporates in our solipsistic pain.

II. VISIBLE OPPRESSION: "BY THE RIVERS OF BABYLON WE SAT AND WEPT" (PSALM 137)

In Ps 137, the sense of abandonment, frustration, and attrition are strong. This is why the use of lamentation is of primary importance, not only because it offers an outlet but especially because it is a lamentation before someone else. The ecological category that triggers that process of dialogue with pain, which becomes a process of remembrance, memory, and prayer in this psalm, are the rivers of Babylon. Pain is not only a psychological experience. In Ps 137, it is also a communitarian and ecological event. The awareness, not only personal or communal but also connected with nature, is thus an ecological awareness, already an antidote to mitigate pain. Resisting and fighting pain individualistically paradoxically perpetuates it. It is this wholistic awareness of pain that pushes and drives us into relationships, into recognition of others, and especially into recognition of others' recognition of us. Recognition is more than being perceived. It has to do with the recognition of our desire to be desired, says psychoanalyst Massimo Recalcati[9]—not of others taking note of our pain but of ourselves as desiring people. Lamentation is an ecological experience; sitting by the figurative rivers of Babylon is a first step in remembering that we are relational beings. Ecological relations help us understand what we are and what we could be through an honest dialogue with the pain that is never ours alone. Ours is always part of a bigger pain, that of a community, that of our ecosystem, that of other species.

Jordan Scott, Canadian poet, reminds us that rivers are our allies, not only to think differently but also to be able to say what we are in alternative ways.[10] Rivers are spaces for communication with others but also with us, with our deepest selves. Rivers allow us to find ourselves by communicating with others, by offering a larger perspective for better personal flourishing. Herman Hesse described Sidharta's own conversion and return to life by learning to listen to the apparently mute river he carelessly saw every day. The mystery and complexity of life was revealed to Sidharta by the river that he was no longer used to listening to—but that he learned to listen

9. Recalcati, *Legge del desiderio*.
10. Scott, *Io parlo come un fiume*, 3–12.

Part I: Compulsions and Sublimations

to with the help of his friend, a boatman. Vasudeva, the boatman, taught him to listen to the river, and from that listening, learn to speak again the correct and essential words of life: "Om,"[11] the "nameless," the "perfect," without which every life is too empty of essential experiences or too full of unnecessary things.

Rivers remind us of our common belonging to humankind, writes Peruvian novelist José Maria Arguedas in *Deep Rivers*, his book about the contradictory and paradoxical history of his own country, Peru.[12] Rivers do not have and do not create borders. Rivers belong to everyone. They cross borders and make dialogue possible between the human groups that settle on their banks. For wanting instead to misuse rivers, which belong to all, through their monopolization and privatization, Babylon was defeated by Cyrus, precisely because of the detour of the Euphrates. Because of one river, the Euphrates, Babylon created her greatness. But by the same river she was defeated. This unstoppable fluidity of rivers was taken as a philosophical metaphor by Heraclitus to describe every human journey made up of contrasting and opposing situations that flow into the same river, that is and is no longer the same an instant later.[13] Let us now briefly comment on the three stanzas of this psalm and the oppression and discomfort they describe.

a. "The philanthropic ogre":[14] "They asked us for songs, those who oppressed us" (verse 1)

A surreal scene is described in this first stanza (verses 1–3). Hebrews have been deported to a foreign land as the fruit not only of a military defeat but also a cultural and religious defeat. The invading power thinks it can dispose of the victims in every way and manner. In its arrogance, it considers itself the absolute master of those it has conquered, and it exercises this domination through various strategies. The first is certainly brute force. No servant, slave, conquered, or deported individual is supposed to be treated well. The arrogance and non-compliance of the conquering power bears down on the oppressed with aggression and oppression. No one chooses

---

11. "Om" is Sanskrit word meaning absolute, perfect, ineffable.
12. Arguedas, *Fiumi profondi*, 4–16.
13. Nietzsche, *Twilight of the Idols*, 16, 17; on Heraclitus and the metaphor of the river, see also the two courses Heidegger did on Heraclitus in 1943 and 1944: Heidegger, *Eraclito*.
14. Paz, *Ogro filantrópico*.

one's oppressor, or if he does, it is done under duress. That is why the oppressor, gentle or swaggering, always makes the weight of his oppression unconditional and without remorse.

The second strategy tries to legitimize that abusive power. Max Weber distinguished between oppression as "macht" (power) and oppression as "herrschaft" (domination).[15] While the first is visible and swaggering, the second is hidden, even kind. *Herrschaft* has been translated into English as "authority" and "domination." "Domination" highlights elements of power and legitimacy that are comingled in the concept, as well as the concept of the asymmetrical power relationship. This second form of oppression imposes itself not by force but symbolically, through an ideological way of conceiving abusive power as necessary, even benevolent. It is what Octavio Paz, Mexican Nobel in literature, calls "el ogro filantrópico" ("the philanthropic ogre"), speaking of the bureaucratic and oppressive state.[16] This second process occurs only by stigmatizing its victims and describing them as irredeemable beasts that can only be redeemed with the all-encompassing paternalistic favor of the oppressor. Here resides the ambivalence of many entities and institutions, which, by helping, wear out, and by granting, rob. Helping institutions often have this strange mix of generosity and oppression, attention and disrespect, interest and exploitation, kindness and sadism, salvation and destruction. Not for nothing the first modern generous institution, the Westphalian State, which is a direct ancestor of today's nations, was originally described by Hobbes as a leviathan. The leviathan is in fact the first modern "philanthropic ogre." And, unfortunately, many churches in the large and transversal span of religious profiles are its more spiritual and ideological incarnations.

Indeed, once in Babylon, deportees were not always obliged into forced labor. Smart oppressors find ways of being kind and understanding, even though in limited and circumstantial manners. Babylonian oppressive power was articulated also as a paternalistic power with a benevolent face that recognized in the deportees some skills, such as those of singing. Those solicited songs, though, were certainly not songs of liberation but songs that implicitly perpetuated the deportees' oppression. Those songs that the Babylonians asked the Jews to sing at the rivers of Babylon were manipulated to reinforce the power of the oppressors. Alienation did not disappear with those songs but insidiously prolonged it through aesthetic

---

15. Weber, *Economy and Society*.
16. Paz, *Ogro filantrópico*.

sublimation. Behind those requested songs were hidden irony, distrust, contempt, and mockery on the part of the oppressors, as when a tourist naively asks for a photo with a caged exotic animal or a differently dressed Indigenous woman. We find here the naive and, at the same time, contemptuous concern for the oppressed, coupled with the cynical claim to give him a respite—a gratification that doesn't change anything but leaves the oppression as it was before, if not worse. The "philanthropic ogre," to borrow Octavio Paz's metaphor again, makes it seem that the oppressive process is not so bad, not so evil—that the oppressor is good, kind, and generous—and sometimes appears impatient, which is the fault of the oppressed who, in one way or another, irritate and anger them. In a process of abuse and oppression, the terms are reversed. The oppressor is the offended one, and the victim is always the one who provokes and vexes. For this reason, the first stanza of this psalm symbolically describes a process of oppression that is difficult not only to unmask but also to dismantle because of the ambivalence of the devious and Machiavellian oppressive power.

b. "The temptation to fail"[17]: "How could we sing songs of the Lord in a foreign land?" (verse 4)

Among the deportees in Babylon, the temptation to sing is strong, as a mechanism to sublimate pain and longing. Singing and context, however, must go together. One does not sing just for the sake of singing. Singing and music are great instruments of protest if they consider their own context. Different contexts demand different kinds of singing. A song that is legitimate in one context may no longer be legitimate in another. Decontextualized singing could simply serve as a mechanism for validating and perpetuating oppression. In the same way, many of the church's hymns and songs today have become mere legitimators of the weariness, exhaustion, and lethargy produced by churches themselves and by their theology. We always have the songs we merit, and we merit the songs we have. For this reason, there should always be a beneficial asymmetry, contrast, even divergence between the songs we sing and the theology we profess. Singing is not only expressive of what we have, it also contests what we have and the way we have it. Singing is not only a docile alternative witness but also a provocative main theological contestation. In this sense, singing must not be submitted to theology and to its orthodoxy as a kind of aesthetic

---

17. Ribeyro, *Temptation of Failing*.

handmaid. Theology needs to be submitted to singing as an atypical way of doing theology "on the way," as Hans Urs Von Balthasar reminds us in his "theological aesthetics."[18]

This is why the reflection of the deportees in Babylon, questioning the function of their singing in an oppressive context, opens a larger perspective in which "musical cultural analysis" flanks the experience of "musical performance." True worship requires a theology and a philosophy of worship as much as singing for the oppressors critically required a philosophy of oppression in Babylon—a reflection that individuates and measures the profile of the final recipients of the benefits of singing. This is not only a debate between the oppressors and their sacred rituals but also a debate between the customary habits and music of the oppressed that indirectly could be used by the oppressor to prolong oppression. The cultural and musical heritage of people has often been recovered and used by the conquering powers to keep them in oppression under the cover of a necessary use of their own history and civil and religious rituals. For instance, the West's interest in the Middle East, Edward Said reminds us, should satisfy middle easterners because it should give them a sense of recognition and even respect from the West.[19] Instead, the opposite happens because the creation of a new science about the Middle East, Said observes, is done all for the use and consumption of the West and its power structures, epistemology, and military. This recognition oppresses because it recognizes only partially and only in function of reinforced subalternity in benefit of the oppressors.

French West Indian psychiatrist and Marxist philosopher Frantz Fanon, in his book *The Wretched of the Earth*, reminds us that this perverse mechanism of partial recognition of the subaltern, the submissive and the exploited, is certainly not only present in the political and social sphere.[20] Unfortunately, the same mechanism is articulated in spheres that are less suspect but serve as de facto oppressive environments, such as religious communities and families. Hence, the need to give not a partial and circumscribed reading of the good things that happen here and there, but rather to be able to understand the overall direction and perspective of groups and events and clearly discern both their oppressive drift or their liberating character. Even a kind and well-intentioned environment may serve as a context that validates and endorses abuse and oppression.

18. Balthasar, *Glory of God*, 17–127.
19. Said, *Orientalism*, 9–31.
20. Fanon, *Wretched of the Earth*.

c. When the oppressed become oppressors:[21] "Daughter of Babylon, blessed is he who seizes your infants and dashes them against the rocks" (verses 8, 9)

Oppression, unfortunately, does not end easily. It tends to prolong and update itself in unexpected ways and forms. What is described as liberation is unfortunately often the birthing act of new forms of oppression. Not only are new forms of oppression possible, but what is even more worrying and paradoxical is that many oppressions emerge in the very bosom of liberatory processes that are insufficiently supervised and assessed. Not even virtues can easily be given a green light to proceed unsupervised. On the contrary, the euphoria of virtues, like the euphoria of liberation, often leads to new forms of alienation and oppression precisely by virtue of the enthusiasm they initially trigger.

The oppressed Jew described in this psalm, like every oppressed person, has an ambivalent character. On the one hand, he is a victim and therefore needs commiseration and compassion. On the other hand, though, he must be kept under eye, for the victim who suffers can easily become dangerous in the very the act of articulating his own liberation. Oppressed people can easily become oppressors with the alibi of working for their own protection and survival, observes Homi Bhabha, because every process of oppression as much as that of liberation is always an ambivalent event.[22] For this reason, it is not enough to implement courageous actions for liberation. We also need, as we are reminded in this psalm, spaces for reflection. In the third stanza, we do not find a recipe for what must be done, but rather a tremendous description of the bullying and eventual destruction of the oppressed by those who have been liberated. Liberation is never over until all people reach the same status. It is up to us to evaluate and filter what is described in this psalm. One possible lesson is precisely this: the oppressed, often and in deferred ways, prolong oppression by creating other victims and other kinds of oppression once they are liberated. In this psalm, we find the infants of Edom and Babylon ending up "crushed against the wall" in the thoughts and desires of the liberated persons. The fact that this revenge is described as happening only in the thoughts and desires of liberated people makes things even worse because it's more difficult to erase evil and revenge from minds and hearts.

---

21. McGibbon, *Oppression*, 3–16.
22. Bhabha, *Location of Culture*, 121–31.

III. PARADOXICAL OPPRESSION: "THE ACHIEVEMENT SOCIETY"[23]

This psalm narrates an oppression in other times, in some ways worse because it was visible and was structured in such a way that it could not be overthrown by single individuals. It was therefore suffered from below, and being vertically structured, it was almost impossible to dismantle. The paradox is that today, in the historical period of individual freedom and constitutionally guaranteed rights, oppression has not disappeared but has changed appearance. This is articulated now horizontally and is not imposed from above but starts from below. For this reason, it is less visible and, consequently, its overthrow becomes even more difficult. We could qualify this oppression, to update this psalm, with three characteristics: hidden, self-generated, and productive.

First, today's oppression tends to be hidden—hidden for several reasons. It is often covered by great efficiency, a fact that prevents it from being detected, but even more fundamentally because contemporary oppression is tied to the space–time structure that modernity has chosen as the foundation of its project. As Aaron Y. Gourevitch says, modernity starts when time/history is chosen as its pivotal category.[24] This bet on time will naturally lead to the speeding up of all the activities we do and the very way we live, thus creating an extreme acceleration that is not only considered legitimate but even becomes a necessary virtue. So much so that, according to Hartmut Rosa, this has become overtime attrition and unconscious, self-produced alienation from being a supreme virtue by the mechanism of "the heterogenesis of ends."[25] But unlike other kinds of alienations that were sectorial, this "temporal alienation," which only considers things as noble and worthy that are quick and dynamic, cuts across all categories of people and groups.

It is a perfectly democratic alienation because it is universal. We don't need to be atheistic or agnostic to be touched by it. It's enough to believe or to attend a church. In other words, one needs only to be modern or post-modern, secular or believer, to be conditioned and deformed by this new kind of alienation. We all live in this "syndrome of haste," or in what Giacomo Marramao[26] calls "dromo-mania."[27] Taking a phrase from Shake-

---

23. Chicchi, *Società della prestazione*, 19–44.
24. Gourevitch, "Postface."
25. Rosa, *Alienation and Acceleration*.
26. Marramao, *Passione del presente*, 100–105.
27. "Dromo-mania" is defined as "obsession with speed."

speare's *Hamlet*, he describes it as an "off-axis time." The linear time that saved us from routine and slowness has subsequently been transformed into the unconscious executioner within ourselves, who oppresses us with a structural and hidden oppression, and from which it becomes impossible to free ourselves because it is also the guarantor of our very subsistence and our greatest achievements.

Second, ours is an autogenous oppression. From being heteronomous and exogenous, oppression has become endogenous and linked to our own autonomy. We have internalized those expectations that, in previous historical periods, others and God had of us. We have become the most implacable judge of what we try to do and achieve. The internalized norms, complicit with our own will, consider that we are never enough. From a "surveillance society," we have moved to an "achievement society," in which all individuals have become their own entrepreneur and judge by nurturing a chain of expectations in a continuous crescendo that comes down on us inexorably and constantly.

Performance, initially desired by us, later has become an iron imposition on us by a context we no longer control. That softer, more indirect control, seemingly chosen by us from below, with minimal, friendly, and innocent initial pressure, finally covers and crushes us like a continuous and intransigent shadow that, in the long run, wears down the spontaneity, lightness, and initiative of our bodies, making them exhausted, tired, and disenchanted.

Third, today's oppression is productive. Whereas past oppression tended to create unproductive work precisely because it was articulated without the concurrence of the will and enthusiasm of the oppressed, today, those who are oppressed are consenting and willing. They choose and like what, on another level, oppresses them. Not knowing that the subsequent attrition stems from their own industriousness and performance, they think that the overcoming of undesired discomfort and weariness depends on increased performance. This paradoxical fact and misinterpretation keeps feeding their attrition even more by feeding their performative work. Weariness, radical activism, is taken as the solution for the anomalies it creates. So, more of the supposed correcting and healing activism creates, in fact, more weariness, and more weariness automatically demands more activism. Our achievement society is stuck in a vicious circle that it is unable to see and to break down.

In fact, compulsion to action is described as a virtue. Today, being busy and always doing something is regarded as nobility of spirit, involvement, and responsibility. Not only that, its problematic nature is not perceived; it's even proposed as the model to be followed. We all suppose and affirm within ourselves that doing is always a virtue and is better than not doing something. Laziness, on the other hand, is the "mother (source) of all evils," as Byung-Chul Han described the implicit manifesto of our "achievement societies."[28] In achievement societies, doing, and doing more and more, is not only ethically virtuous but also anthropologically necessary. Committed and conviction-filled activism keeps us busy, producing results that justify not only what we do but also who we are. This produces the mechanicalness, sold as regularity, and compulsion, smuggled in as responsibility, of contemporary humanity's actions.

This strange mix of performance and weariness, besides being psychological, affects our bodies. Faced with the sight of well-fed, beautiful, high-performing bodies, we have the impression that bodies today are better than in any other historical period. Proof of this is the incredible increase in the average life span, which, in some countries, is more than eighty years. Yet, this is not necessarily so. A sense of strength and of precariousness coexist in our bodies. We have this dual sensation of unstoppable dynamism and monotony that needs to be overcome. The agony and anonymity of bodily sense imperceptibly triggers a compulsion to action. Our bodies seem to be fine only in relation to increasing and sophisticated activism.

Hence, the feeling that our bodies are drugged, stimulated, and exploited, not by someone outside but by our inability to stop and welcome a meaning that is offered as a gift. The paradox is that, in contemporary society, we have dynamic, highly performing, and "efficient" bodies. But, at the same time, we behave as worn out, tired, exploited, over-controlled, and "deficient" bodies. Our bodies become performing machines without "*eros*."[29] Without *eros* not only because they are without vital drive, captive solely to routine patterns of performance, but without *eros* because our bodies are isolated. Byung-Chul Han reminds us that the body, a healthy body, must necessarily be vital. And it can only be vital in relationships.

> Eros is about the Other in the emphatic sense, which does not allow itself to be resolved in the regime of the ego.[30]

---

28. Han, "Beyond Disciplinary Society," 8–11.
29. Han, *Eros in agonia*, 4–19.
30. Han, *Eros in agonia*, 6.

Part I: Compulsions and Sublimations

Therefore, the body has been lost not in forgetfulness, indifference, or abandonment but, paradoxically, it is in constant concern, solicitation, and care. This is "body-olatry," a compulsive and daily worship of one's own body. This type of worship detaches us from the rest of life and from others who are the epitome of health, because health is not reducible to functionality but is essentially possible only in relationships. The paradox is that this quantitative overconcentration hides a qualitative inattention of the body. In fact, we have multiple, sophisticated, and constant measurements of the body, continually updated (quantitative body). But, at the same time, we completely miss the immensurability of the body (qualitative body), which symbols and rituals of the past evoked without claiming to control. We have developed a science but not a wisdom of the body. Our bodies are oppressed and exploited by performative strategies set up by ourselves.

The external oppressor has become internal. From "shame-centered-communities," which are group-based, we have moved to "guilt-centered-societies," which are based only on individuals, according to anthropologist Ruth Benedict,[31] proving that it is not others but ourselves who create excessive expectations, and thus attrition and weariness.[32] This attrition is created by an obsession with efficiency, work, and discipline. Work, Walter Benjamin states in his eleventh thesis on history, is the new "messiah."[33] We need hard-working individuals and hard-working bodies. A critique of human and ethical laziness and indolence, typical of our time, cannot therefore be articulated without a critique of work and performance. And religions, Adventism included, which should have resisted this cultural trend, have instead helped in interiorizing this performative model. For this reason, beyond an initial and limited benefit, today's religions, through the same mechanisms, are responsible for the weariness of persons and bodies through legitimized activism.

The problem is not only linked to excessive work but to work that also becomes oppressive. The situation is complex because, along with a critique of work and the conditions of work, we must at the same time fight for more work and secure decent work still unavailable for enormous sectors of our society. But the defense of work cannot proceed without a critique of the idolatry of work as a condition of alienation and oppression in contemporary society. This critique of work, which does not coincide

---

31. Benedict, *Chrysanthemum and the Sword*, 12–32.
32. Benedict, *Chrysanthemum and the Sword*, 15.
33. Benjamin, "Thesis on the Philosophy," 196–208.

with a denial of work as an important dimension of today's anthropology, must necessarily be brought into relationship, as Ps 137 suggests, with play and singing—in a word, with aesthetics.

As in Babylon, now in our present societies, there is a strange mix of wearisome labor and sublimated singing. The Babylonians who asked the Hebrew exiles to sing were certainly not to give them freedom through their songs but to, on the one hand, give the impression of empathy and generosity and, on the other hand, to neutralize the power of songs by granting only a folkloristic form of it, as is the case today. There was not so much singing, so much music, and so much dancing as there is today in our achievement societies. But paradoxically, today's exuberant and impressive amount of music is not at the center of life nor work but only on the periphery, the margins.

We are allowed to play music only after we have worked, not during working hours. Making music while working is not only impossible because of the rhythm and discipline required but rather because it's forbidden. It would slow down work and prevent us from producing adequately. So, music and singing are scheduled for after we have worked and secured the production needed. What matters here is work, not singing. Whatever else, music included, can be partially tolerated and welcome in so far as it facilitates and guarantees the articulation of efficient and productive work. Here, music becomes important because work tires and wears out. When we need a break, music, in its various forms, becomes important and necessary to recharge, to refresh tired workers so that they can work better. Music, so conceived and implemented, does not change work, but it is used to confirm and prolong autogenic oppression and alienation, bound and dependent of performative and compulsive action paradigms. Music becomes an appendix of work, used in function of work. As in Babylon, the singing required of the Jews was not intended to change the forced labor and thus was not intended to be liberating.

Ours are not "celebrating societies" or, as Erich Fromm calls pre-modern societies, "orgiastic societies."[34] In "festivity-centered-societies," people work—a lot. But work is at the service of life and the group through rituals, symbols, and festivals that split the linearity and mechanicalness of work and make it become relationship, gift, cooperation, and worship. Our "civilized" societies are credited with introducing order and efficiency, but at the expense of shared joy and personal flourishing. We are well composed, even

---

34. Fromm, *Art of Loving*, 14–35.

efficient, but sad, worn-out workers. We have excluded celebration, play, and song as residual elements in the chain of life. We have banned them from real life, from its center. We have intense but peripheral spaces for singing. They are not central. We have, nonetheless, not excluded them completely because, without them, life and work would be impossible. By being marginalized, they don't transform us but only give us limited spaces and moments to evade and escape the iron cage of omnipresent, disciplinary work.

It is no coincidence that Hannah Arendt recalled that in pre-modern cultures, particularly in the Greek culture, there were different ways of describing human action (labor, action, work).[35] These distinctions have disappeared today and we are left with only one form that matters—precisely, "work" understood as mechanical labor. Contemporary anthropology is a typical modern anthropology of "homo faber." And "homo faber," in his obsession with performance, automatically uses those tools that could correct him (song, music, dancing) to reinforce and not to dismantle his obsession. And just as he does with music, he also does with religion. Modern religions do not correct the performative obsession of contemporary humanity but, unfortunately, reinforce it. And on this issue, Adventism is at the forefront.

For this reason, unconscious, transversal, and chronic oppression we contemporaries create for ourselves and for others transform and deform everything we touch. It's not what we do but how we do it that matters. And our "how" is structurally impregnated with this performative obsession, even when we speak of God, the Bible, philanthropy, giving, love, or worship. Civilized and efficient societies, as much as the correspondent and parallel religious communities generated by them, are certainly not perverse in themselves. They are an option in the span of sociocultural forms that have emerged in history. But they are not unique, and they are not necessarily perfect. They are not unique in the sense that there are other possible social and cultural configurations. They are not perfect in the sense that it is not their incoherence but the very coherence with their own patterns that create anomalies.

Anomalies are not subsequent drifts of the wrong applications of a perfect model. Every good model generates, from the beginning, its own typical anomalies. And what happens with cultural models happens also with churches. Adventism automatically generates typical Adventist anomalies that will not and cannot disappear. Paradoxically, this fact represents

---

35. Arendt, *Human Condition*, 136–74.

a blessing. Social and religious anomalies, as much as fever or pain, are our allies because they remind us that there is not a perfect model. Pushed by them (fever or pain as signs and symptoms), a good body can take up again the road of health, which is never a state but a process. Even the so-called biblical model is only perfect if it accepts and admits its own unilateralism and asymmetries. The Bible is a unilateral book; its perfection resides precisely in this. This fact, therefore, applies also to Adventism. The structural unilateralism of Adventism doesn't mean that Adventism is wrong, false, or inappropriate. It simply implies that Adventism is necessarily human and necessarily unilateral. Being unilateral and incomplete is a blessing that, if managed with wisdom and humility, could preserve Adventism from bibliolatry and ecclesiolatry, two plagues that have deformed and decimated some of the best expressions of Christianity in church history.

Coming back to oppression, this paradoxical mix of "oppression" and "singing" (the intertwined motives in Ps 137) and its innovative and counterintuitive modern update (articulated as "obsessive work" and "numbing singing" typical of our "achievement societies") doesn't depend on singular choice or communitarian indications. Before that choice, singular or corporative, there is a cultural model that precedes our awareness and conditions and influences whatever we do and think. No cultural model is perverse or virtuous in itself, or anthropologically and religiously neutral. That structural model needs to be understood to know what can be done—particularly, what is advisable and desirable for individuals and believers to do. We will characterize this cultural performative model with three structural traits: disembedding, intellectualization, and emotional illiteracy.

a. "Disembedding"

Anthony Giddens characterizes our achievement societies as typical "disembedded societies," i.e., as societies, which by separating and detaching elements that until then were structurally united, have created a remarkable dynamism, efficiency, and progress.[36] Charles Taylor also considers "disembedding" as the main explanatory mechanism of our contemporary world.[37] Taylor says that, until about five hundred years ago, humanity naturally confronted itself with external events having mysterious, transcendent dimensions: natural disasters, good or bad spirits, miraculous formulas and

36. Giddens, *Consequences of Modernity*, 5–15.
37. Taylor, *Secular Age*, 25–89.

Part I: Compulsions and Sublimations

potions, vital fluids and relics, the extraordinary in the everyday. A colorful "enchanted" world easily unhindered and penetrated what he calls "porous self" (pre-modern humans), who, being nurtured from the outside, easily identified with it. Between self and the external world, there was absolute continuity; they were one and the same. The natural world represented the self well, just as the self was perfectly describable in natural terms. Meaning filtered from the world outside automatically. Humanity was in continuity with the group, with God, and with nature. The "porous self" was structurally an expression of a relational anthropology.

Everything changed with the arrival of modernity, helped by the Latin-Western version of Christianity and, above all, by Protestantism, as Max Weber suggests.[38] What counted now was inwardness, personal faith, and living prayer hidden in the heart. With the Enlightenment, the same rejection takes on a new face: the world, which had been obvious to the "porous self" for centuries, is condemned as a false world. The external world, described by pre-moderns, is described as the enchanted and illusory production of a world that doesn't exist and is forged only by an immature and superstitious interiority. Such a diagnosis marks the victory of a new anthropology, that of the "buffered self." The new, well-shielded self is critical and distrustful of any exteriority. Individualism, before being social, is anthropological and necessarily carries with it the idea, obvious to us, of history as development or progress, which is in fact a kind of compensation for the lack of relations. Once the traditional multiple relations of pre-modern humanity have been abandoned, the modern self immediately starts creating new relations and a new world that will be no longer be regarded as received but man-made. Modern humanity has an intrinsically constructivist spirit. Western thought perceives itself as superior to that of other ages and cultures and declares itself autonomous and free from the ancient fears that bound it to nature. One of the great differences between us and our predecessors is that we live with a much firmer perception of the boundary separating the self from the rest (i.e., the nonself). We are *shielded* selves. Our perception of us and the world has totally changed.

This hyperconcentration on self would therefore not be entirely virtuous and would not even be a sign of a conscious choice but would represent the unconscious and subdued search for a bond that we lack—and that, not being able to find it in others, we find with our own activities. Activism becomes a compensatory mechanism for the loss of others. This is a typical narcissistic mechanism. Pragmatism would be precisely this substitution

---

38. Weber, *Protestant Ethic*.

of others with the worship of one's own actions; and, if ever others serve, they serve only as spectators. We are thus faced with a typical mechanism of compensation and fixation in which subjects are incapable of changing the goals of their own drive. Pragmatism would be the sign of a loss, not only of others but ultimately also the loss of ourselves. And the society of performance,[39] the one that erects as a model maximum efficiency and results, would be nothing more than the accentuation of this isolation and solitude present as a tendency in contemporary anthropology, since its very beginning in the "buffered self" described by Taylor.[40]

b. "Intellectualization of Life"[41]

Georg Simmel describes achievement societies by introducing a new perspective: the analysis of our cities and some typical categories linked to it. Categories like money, fashion, art, housing, sexuality, or prostitution[42] (typical categories of modern civilization) have an enormous impact on us moderns. These categories help us to be what we are. But they also deform what we are by excluding, for instance, the ability to enjoy and celebrate the capacity to be in touch with our feelings and emotions. Behind highly performative individuals, we find a kind, respectful, morally reliable, but also an emotionally illiterate, apathetic, and passionless person. Elena Pulcini calls the performative individual of our time "the individual without passions,"[43] as much as Eva Illouz calls our time the time of "cold intimacies."[44]

But let's come back to Simmel, and particularly his description of modern big cities (metropolis) and their impact on our capacity to work and sing.[45] Simmel is an acute, sharp, and meticulous observer of Berlin, as Walter Benjamin is of Paris[46] with the intent of describing modernity starting from some European metropolis.[47] Simmel argues that the characteristic of the modern way of living is incorporated and perfectly visible

39. Chicchi, *Società della prestazione*, 8–23.
40. Taylor, *Secular Age*.
41. Simmel, *Metropoli*, 39–39.
42. Simmel, *On Individuality*.
43. Pulcini, *Individual Without Passions*, 1–9.
44. Illouz, *Cold Intimacies*, 11–32.
45. Frisby, *Fragments of Modernity*.
46. Benjamin, *Arcades Project*.
47. Rafele, *Métropole*, 7–19.

Part I: Compulsions and Sublimations

in today's cities. Humanity has created modern cities, and modern cities determine what modern individuals are. Most of today's population lives in big cities. And even small villages function as small cities, with the same mechanisms. Following Simmel, let's mention and briefly comment on two main transformations modern cities produce on humanity and the way bottom-up and autogenic oppression is configured today.

According to Simmel, the first important anthropological modification determined by the cities we live in is the "intellectualization of life."[48] A distinctive trait of modern cities is speed. Scenarios, contexts, interlocutors, visual and audio stimuli, etc., change continuously and very quickly. For this reason, there is a demand and a big capacity for adaptation and an enormous amount of flexibility and rapidity. Of the various mental and psychological capacities and functions we possess, intellect is the fastest, most adaptable, and most flexible. The only way to survive this extremely demanding, stimulating, changeable, and heterogeneous new context is by using and reinforcing our intellect, which among all our other capacities is the best fit for this. The result is that we all, more than "pragmatics," are rather "intellectuals." In his booklet *Metropolis and Mental Life*, Simmel reminds us that today, diffuse pragmatism depends on and is built up on this transversal "intellectualization" of life.[49] Certainly, this is not a speculative intellectualization but a pragmatic one. Simmel adds that the flexibility and speed of intellect is determined by the fact that intellect is a superficial dimension of our being. Only what is superficial and lacks in depth can effectively change and rapidly adapt.

c. "Obliteration of Emotions"[50]

The second trait of life linked to modern cities and narrowly dependent of the first one, according to Simmel, is the "obliteration of emotions." Emotions are slow and ambivalent because they are rooted in the deep dimensions of our being. For this reason, emotional illiteracy, psychological apathy, or affective indifference are not tardive anomalies of modern humanity but original components of modern anthropology linked to the cities we have created. In other words, city life requires that we, in a civil and unconscious way, obliterate our emotions. We couldn't otherwise live

48. Simmel, *Metropoli*, 2–14.
49. Simmel, *Metropoli*, 37.
50. Simmel, *Metropoli*, 36–37.

intensively the numberless social or technical opportunities we constantly face in big cities. That would be too psychologically demanding. In order to survive, we need to cool down our emotions and allow them to become standard. We cannot love intensively every person we meet in the metro or at the market. We just learn, by necessity, to be indifferent while still trying to remain polite—respectful but detached.

We will love intensively only a restricted group of people, those we have chosen: our family and friends. We couldn't do otherwise. But since events are never completely under control, the unexpected happens. It's not the deep love and affection of our restricted little group that partially emigrates and positively contaminates our standard interaction with unknown people on the bus or in the market. Rather, the opposite happens, writes Jungian psychoanalyst Luigi Zoja in his book *The Death of the Neighbor*.[51] The standard affective attitude made by cooling our emotions, typically in public spaces (markets, stadiums, airports, etc.), takes over the spaces of emotional intimacy. We start treating people dear to us with the same standard emotional attitude reserved to people in common places. "The neighbor is symbolically dead," says Zoja.[52] Social quantity has killed anthropological quality. But the process doesn't end here. After the common public and our intimate circle has been standardized, we consequently become standardized and reified in our emotions. The result is a new anthropology of the efficient by emotionally illiterate individuals. The city, then the school, the hospital, the church, and unfortunately also our families have inherited and copied this emotional standard anthropological version of the efficient person. By this, they have transformed us into apathetic, unfeeling, unemotional individuals who, to compensate for this emotional loss, need to increase the things they do. Action becomes compulsion, and compulsion behaves as sublimation.

We could say that the ambivalence described in Ps 137 concerning oppression and liberation, even if expressed in different terms, still belongs to our reality today. No human process of oppression or liberation is linear, clear, and univocal. For this reason, we are like the Hebrews oppressed in Babylon, even if differently, as much as their Babylonian oppressors, who, even ignoring their paradoxical oppression, lived this ambivalence and were determined by it. For the same reason we cannot ignore that, even in our churches or families, the virtuous initiatives and habits we have created

---

51. Zoja, *Morte del prossimo*, 7–21.
52. Zoja, *Morte del prossimo*, 12.

with effort, coherence, and conviction may also create oppression and weariness in our souls, bodies, and minds. This typical intellectualization of city life corresponds, in parallel, to the intellectualization of our churches and our religious lives by the same mechanisms and, unfortunately, with the same effects.

We may try to be different from others doctrinally and theologically, but anthropologically, we are very similar. We belong to the same historical period with its virtues and imbalances. To ignore this fact not only pushes us into false assumptions but also into an impolite and ungracious contempt and disdain of others. Whatever we do theologically and ethically, we Adventists suffer the same medical diseases and social anomalies. The "intellectualization of life" and the "obliteration of emotions" are as much a part of Adventism as they are of nonbelievers and those who believe differently. This anthropological situation cannot be changed with more prayer or by reading *The Great Controversy*. I cannot pray to become black if I am white, or to be Chinese if I am Peruvian. It doesn't mean that I cannot resist the bad part of this cultural conditioning. I can resist it only if I recognize the positive elements of that culture. Cultural resistance is impossible without cultural acceptance, and the only way of distinguishing both is by getting to know culture and avoiding being imprisoned in the Bible. Reading the Bible alone without interest and emotion for the world the Bible speaks about is not only bad but dangerous.

d. Orthopathy: Slowness for Relations

It is not enough to have the right ideas about God and life (orthodoxy) and to add to this religious virtuosity correct and coherent practices (orthopraxis). We need to also be emotionally healthy. Therefore, a third theological register is needed—not to cancel the other two but to build upon them. Something that takes better care of a specific human dimension has been particularly neglected and atrophied by our contemporary way of life.

This is what "slow Adventism" means in the title of this book. It is not only a matter of slowing down to keep the same attitudes, registers, interests, and priorities as before. As Harmut Rosa reminds us, we don't answer to the "alienating acceleration" with a simple "deceleration."[53] Deceleration is not a goal in itself, only an instrument to change our focus from resources to happiness, from quantity to quality, from programs to people, from ideas

---

53. Rosa, "If Our Problem Is Acceleration," 7–36.

to events, from seriality to exceptions, from linearity to complexity—or as Italian philosopher Roberto Esposito says, from "things" to "persons."[54] The speeding up of our way of life, as described by Simmel and linked to the cities we have built, has not only led to the "intellectualization of modern life" but also to what Axel Honneth describes as the "reification of reality."[55] Olivier Roy calls it "the flattening of the world,"[56] where the unique king and determinant tool has become what Charles Taylor describes as the omnipotent and omnipresent "instrumental reason."[57]

Unfortunately, and unwillingly, much Adventist doctrine and practice, witnessing and administration, is led by and deeply dependent on this "instrumental reason," even though it is covered and edulcorated with typical biblical and Adventist categories and motives.

A "slow Adventism," then, is not only a matter of speed but about understanding that only by slowing down would we be able to get in touch with deep dimensions, which don't emerge at the current pace of living in our typical achievement societies. Our churches, as much as our cities, have become rapid and smart places that work only on the surface of life, unable to go deep into emotions and affects because they are too demanding, too complex, and too contradictory. We cannot be emotionally healthy if we remain on the surface. Even sanctification, understood as a necessary complement to justification, is insufficient. Sanctification in Adventism has become too much of a linear process. Final-events missiology and eschatology detached from the complexity of emotions is insufficient. Feelings and emotions are the thermostat and thermometer of the quality of a faith experience and of witnessing. The problem of a "fast Adventism" is not what it does or doesn't do but rather how it does what it does.

We need a new register that checks the health of our attitudes and emotions beyond the correctness of our doctrines and praxis. This new register is "orthopathy." A true or coherent person could paradoxically be dangerous, not from a legal or penal point of view but from a life-oriented perspective. Mission and eschatology, as much as Bible reading, are essentially for transmitting life. All other elements are secondary.

---

54. Esposito, *Persone e le cose*, 3–35.
55. Honneth, *Verdinglichung*, 12–32.
56. Roy, *Appiattimento del mondo*, 15–31.
57. Taylor, *Malaise of Modernity*, 4–21.

Part I: Compulsions and Sublimations

"Orthopathy" is the healthy human and trusting stance and posture toward life, God, and others.[58] Beyond ideas and behavior, which necessarily demand the intervention of reason, will, and awareness, are instead fundamental prerational attitudes linked to affections and emotions. Starting at a prerational level, but not by irrational or arational attitudes, such as deep motions, breathing, and sighing from the bottom of our being, leads us to perceive our incompleteness, vulnerability, and dependence on what is external to us. By feeling that which is outside (neighbor, group, nature, cosmos, or God) as our own, we aspire to reach out and be touched, provoked, and involved. Without losing in this encounter either our specificity or autonomy, we give them both direction, motivation, and desire for relationship.

Orthopathy, so defined, comes near to what Richard Rice calls "belonging." Right doctrines and correct behaviors, writes Rice in his book *Believing, Behaving, Belonging*, are necessary but insufficient for building up a healthy Adventism.[59] We necessarily need a new register. Belonging, in the past considered secondary and accessory, must become our absolute priority. Orthopathy, however, in Rice's analysis, is described almost exclusively in social and ecclesiological terms. Friedrich Schleiermacher, in reaction to the extreme rational and analytical perspective of the Enlightenment (Kant), defined the religious experience, much as Rice would do much later, as necessarily going beyond "believing" and "behaving," reaching a third dimension that could be described also as "belonging." But in contrast to Rice, Schleiermacher's belonging is defined not sociologically or ecclesiologically but in anthropological and mystical terms. He writes in the second of his five discourses on religion,

> In order to take possession of its own domain, religion renounces herewith all claims to whatever belongs to those others and gives back everything that has been forced upon it. It does not wish to determine and explain the universe according to its nature as does metaphysics; it does not desire to continue the universe's development and perfect it by the power of freedom and the divine free choice of a human being as does morals. Religion's essence is neither thinking nor acting, but intuition and feeling.[60]

---

58. This third sense, not necessarily against but beyond the orthodoxy of ideas and orthopraxy of action, is the meaning Bruno Forte ascribes to beauty. See Forte, *Dove va il cristianesimo?*, 75–83.

59. Rice, *Believing, Behaving, Belonging*.

60. Schleiermacher, *On Religion*, 22.

Much has been said about this definition, particularly in evangelical circles. Karl Barth was critical of this definition because it made too humanely immanent what instead needs to be kept transcendent. But in my opinion, Schleiermacher sees this in the right direction, even though his proposal is still too anthropocentric, individualistic, mystical, and exclusionary of doctrinal and moral components that are part, in various degrees and forms, of a healthy religious experience.

In a larger understanding of orthopathy, we find the valorization of bonding, relationship, and alliance—the aspiration for the recomposing of the whole. This is not accomplished by resorting to contractual (rational and conscious) strategies that presuppose a strong and self-sufficient subject who resorts to the group only strategically and transiently. Neither is it by resorting to identitarian strategies that presuppose the strength of the system/group as the guardian and guarantor of the well-being of individuals, which individuals cannot challenge or do without. Orthopathy, which strongly presupposes vulnerability as a new way of being, is critical of the anthropology of the "souverain self," illusorily presupposed by contemporary societies and churches, write Gayatri Spivak and Judith Butler.[61] Orthopathy starts with individuals, from their vulnerability and incompleteness, but goes beyond to something bigger: relations and belonging understood not only sociologically or ecclesiologically but anthropologically and ecologically. Precisely because we are free, we are free for the sake of relationships. There is no freedom outside relationships. The loss of meaning is thus a loss of the other. There is no sense without the other, just as there is no freedom without the other.

Orthopathy, which represents a slow and fast, complex and fragmentary, unitary and paradoxical way of achieving meaning, aims to grasp the vision of totality without possessing it. It pushes toward the intuition of the whole without manipulating it. It promotes the imagination of the complexity of life by renouncing the compulsiveness that claims to order and organize it.

CONCLUSION

Psalm 137 reminds us that personal or community history is never linear; it zigzags and is full of crossroads, junctions, and parallel roads, like rivers.[62] Oppressor and oppressed are never well-defined; clear profiles often blur and

61. Spivak, *Who Sings the Nation-State?*, 46–73.
62. Yao, *Ideal River*.

overlap. Those who are oppressed easily become oppressors and oppressors are already, from the very beginning, victims and oppressed by something naively overlooked and disowned. This does not mean that legal, penal, or ethical clarity is not desirable and reachable. This clarity must be sought and safeguarded as a fundamental ingredient for the organization and survival of human groups. But in a more anthropological realm, knowing that the lines are often unclear or overlapping is nonetheless helpful in practicing tolerance as much as possible while still applying the law in a redemptive sense.

This psalm thus raises some basic questions that are even today difficult both to articulate and to answer: What does it feel like to inhabit a foreign land psychologically, within territories that are instead familiar to us? How is it possible to experience happiness when, at the same time, our basic problems are still not solved? What is the true status of our singing, music, dancing, and worship in our performative churches and families? What do rivers teach us about situations that seem perpetual and never changing? In which sense are rivers, mountains, and nature part of our religious experience and also part of our identity? How and when do virtues and assets, when not monitored and properly assessed, become causes and sources of oppression and alienation?

Taken in this perspective, nature, with the rivers that represent it, is a master at reminding us not only of the transience of the events we experience but also of the overlapping of opposing and contrary elements that we would instead like to keep distinct, according to poet Chandra Candiani.[63] The river comes and goes; it is shallow and deep; it gives life and overwhelms it; it waits for us but also overtakes us. There is often danger hidden in the most innocent things. And life can be reborn from the most warped and crooked things. This is the mystery and complexity of life revealed to Sidharta by the river that he was no longer used to listening to but will learn to do so with the help of the boatman who, in that river, teaches him to find life again and to say again that "Om,"[64] the "nameless," the "perfect," without which all life is too empty or too full.[65] Liberation doesn't always come from action, as achievement societies have made us believe, but also from inactivity, slowness, and contemplation—contemplation of others, of nature, of God. "Be still, and know that I am God" (Ps 46:10) is a counterpoint with respect to the current rhythm of churches and societies that we live in today.

63. Candiani, *Sogni de fiume*, 3–15.
64. "Om" is Sanskrit word meaning absolute, perfect, ineffable.
65. See especially chapters 4 and 5 of part 2 entitled "By the River" and "The Boatman" in Hesse's *Siddhartha*, 107–35.

2

Adventism and the Challenge of Inculturation

HOLZWEGE IS A WELL-KNOWN 1950 book by Martin Heidegger that uses a metaphor from an area dear to him, "The Black Forest" ("Der Schwarzwald").[1] This is a mountainous region in southwest Germany bordering France, renowned for its dense evergreen forests and picturesque villages, which Heidegger used to frequent on long walks. *Holzwege* are thus "the paths in the forest." While in the same forest, each of them proceeds on its own. One may look like another, but they are different. There is no single trail. Many will ultimately make one, but that is a diversified path. Woodsmen and foresters know what it means to be on a track that, by interrupting, diverts, but by diverting, advances. In this sense, Heidegger seems to mean that human thought must not set itself a univocal and compact final goal, much less a final synthesis. On the contrary, it can only proceed as a continuous diversion, as an irreducible wandering. There is thus no single path for reflection, but all paths of thought are eventually legitimate and useful in different stages, ways, and times.

From another side, inculturation, the process of coming near to and taking roots in a culture other than ours, implies not only the capacity to add something to what we have but rather the necessity to transform all

---

1. Heidegger, *Holzwege*.

that we have through these new elements we are assimilating. Inculturation in this sense is not an additive process of identity strengthening but a transformative event of identity flexibilization. For this reason, inculturation implies and requires a partial emptying of what we are in order to be completed by an extrinsic element we don't have. In this sense, inculturation is a kenotic[2] experience. From a typical pragmatic universalist perspective, Adventism got inculturated in Europe as *holzwege*, understood like a structurally diversified way of perceiving and articulating Adventism. Unity didn't disappear but was understood as a polycentric unity, not as a symbiotic or homogeneous one.

But *holzwege* doesn't mean only diversification. It also implies to slowdown the way we do things and the way we learn to be ourselves. *Holzwege*, for this reason slows down our pace and makes mediate what we would like to be immediate, fast, and conclusive. *Holzwege* pushes us to root our identity in a territory through a process that demands time, willingness, understanding, dialogue, and wisdom. As such, *holzwege* is a fitting metaphor for the inculturation of Adventism in Europe. European Adventism, which, like forest paths, represents different and even opposing sensitivities, perceptions, and mentalities. They may overlap, intersect, and confront each other, but they have learned to coexist in tension in the same forest of Adventism, even with a structural and permanent difficulty. This cultural and even theological diversification certainly exists also in other geographical areas, but not with the same intensity, historical rootedness, spread, creativity, and naturalness. This diversification is not traceable to some elite leader, institutional project, or manifesto. It comes from below, from ordinary people, from communities themselves. It exists; it is a given. It's a historical fact. This is Europe—cultural and linguistic polycentrism, and consequently, theological-religious polycentrism—which European Adventism has inherited in its own DNA.

European Adventism is not Adventism in Europe but Adventism transformed by Europe. And this is an asset that we cannot lose. Unfortunately, that is not clear today, even to the European leaders themselves. Adventism, when it comes to Europe, is not aware of this because, when coming from America, it is viewed as a supposedly universal message. It's valid everywhere, relevant everywhere. Adventism is thought of as a socioculturally neutral and

---

2. A Greek term which means "emptying." It appears in the christological hymn of Phil 2:6–11, where it means the giving up of divine glory by the eternal Son of God when he became incarnate.

pure event, both in its inception and also in its destination, where it will be preached. Consequently, Adventism has within itself this historical naivety from the start, from what the Colombian philosopher Santiago Castro-Gómez calls "the hybris [arrogance] of the zero point,"[3] or what Donna Haraway describes as the "god-trick,"[4] understood as a "gaze from nowhere," i.e., the search of an Archimedean point—a fixed pivot from where we can have a neutral and totalizing view of life and reality.

Adventism is supposedly clear to everyone. This is the assumption that accompanies our theology and mission from the very beginning. If someone does not listen, this is not Adventism's problem but the listener's problem. The whole Adventist communication chain, theological and missiological, is perfectly centered on the message and its power at the expense of the recipient. Adventism tends to be a "message-centered" religion, completely heedless of the listener's legitimate questions. These questions are, for Adventism, a disturbance, expressing bad faith and threatening the consistency of a perfect message. That is why our schools of theology emphasize theological repetition rather than theological exploration. That is, we fail to recognize that the earnest pressing of the listener's questions could prolong and refine the essence of our message. Instead, Adventism does not want to confront the struggle to inculturate, to translate itself, to try and settle naturally into a particular territory and its demands.

Adventism compensates for its theological laziness with a pragmatic compulsion. But this pragmatism ends up being an empty repetition of the same. The diversity of places we arrive at is not a problem for us. We speak in Kinshasa, Lima, Kuala Lumpur, Sydney, Berlin, or Rome as if we were speaking in Washington, DC. The failure to inculturate our message into the places where we arrive has not only plagued us but also left our message in its generic and less-than-relevant state. Ours becomes a superficial message that assumes an average, intellectually passive, culturally conformist, and institutionally predictable church member. Despite the proclamations, our impact on some territories has proven to be negligible to nonexistent. This is certainly the case in Europe, and it is even more so at present when Adventism is quickly folding in on itself, doing everything it can to disconnect from outside interlocutors, except when they are in agreement.

However, seen from another perspective, we could paradoxically say that this universalist approach of Adventism in Europe has not succeeded.

3. Castro-Gómez, *Giro decolonial*, 11–32.
4. Haraway, *Simians, Cyborgs, and Women*, 189.

Part I: Compulsions and Sublimations

A denomination that thought it could change Europe by evangelizing it has come out instead transformed by it. In fact, European Adventism is more European than Adventist, and this does not please mainline Adventism that is structurally universalist and disincarnate. In this sense, European Adventism is a healthy exception. And it is so precisely because it is configured as a *holzwege*, a set of sensibilities united by a shared perspective but irreducible to a single interpretation of that perspective. European Adventism is not monolithic from its inception. It not only creates alternatives within itself but is an alternative to world Adventism as well.

To many in the global church, this European Adventism appears as an anomaly to be corrected. There are today in Europe endless missionaries who are zealous and full of ambition. But they are also monotonous and repetitive, predictable and mechanical. They come from various locales: North America, Latin America, Africa, and the borders of Europe itself. They try to convert a European Adventism that is perceived as atypical, anomalous, and even apostate. Its numbers would prove this. In Italy, for example, there are 9,000 Adventists per 60 million inhabitants. In France, 11,000 Adventists per 68 million inhabitants. For 315 million people in South America, there are 2 million Adventists. In the Inter-European-Division (EUD), there are 180,000 Adventists for 340 million people. In the Trans-European-Division (TED), there are only 87,000 Adventists for 205 million people. Numerically, European Adventism is negligible. Some fear for its demise. This, of course, would be proof of its supposed failure. Thus, trying to heal it means leading it back to what "normative" Adventism is in other parts of the world: militant, certain, apocalyptic, and missionary. But above all, it means Adventism should be theologically and institutionally *homogeneous*. European Adventism's supposed anomaly thus would precisely consist in this dispersion and tolerance of different ideas and sensibilities that supposedly hinders its pace and survival—in its being *holzwege*.

It is certainly desirable for European Adventism to strengthen itself numerically to give itself a better prospect of survival. But can this numerical reinforcement guarantee survival without distorting its essence, its being *holzwege*?

This "holzwege-ness," for the European soul and beyond, is more central than we think. It is not only related to diversification of sensibilities and perceptions. More fundamentally, being *holzwege* is related to the very nature of faith and truth. Not surprisingly, a wisdom book like Proverbs reminds us that we must resist the temptation of synthesis. Any synthesis is the basis and presupposition of all pragmatisms, secular and religious, understood as linear and univocal practices. But it could express also an idolatry of compact unity, without fractures. Conversely, wisdom makes its voice heard in the streets, in the alleys, in the crossroads, in the corners of life, where a final and conclusive synthesis is impossible (see Prov 8:2).

For all faith—if it really *is* faith—is always fragmentary, provisional, and on the move, as theologian Mayra Rivera of Harvard University reminds us.[5] God is always transcendent to our syntheses and questions. Ours remains a *holzwege* of questions, intents, desires, and diverse initiatives that try to grasp God. We cannot understand fully, but this does not mean God is unreachable. God will always be beyond our synthesis but still always within reach of our "touch." But that's it, precisely. A touch is a grazing, a partial seeing, and partially perceiving—in essence, a *holzwege*. This is God's transcendence, not that of an unreachable God but the transcendence of one who is touched by our questions and prayers that are always multiple and heterogeneous. Mayra Rivera's answer is that God is not within human grasp but is always within human touch. This is a strikingly relevant concept of God as transcendent within, but transcendence different from the idea of God as far away, outside human life and experience, above the human plane of existence. Rivera instead focuses on transcendence as a relationship and uses it to describe how humans can touch God.

The metaphor of the *holzwege*, which characterizes European Adventism and its inculturation in this territory, is thus not so far from a biblical view of faith as a journey. Theology is always *theologia viatorum*, "theology on the way"—theology that is provisional and fragmented and therefore necessarily diversified and dialogical. Yes, a European Adventism is there, and it is more pertinent than we think, both to the survival of Adventism in Europe and to Adventism worldwide.

---

5. Rivera, *Touch of Transcendence*, 9–31.

3

The Elusiveness of the Particular
On Micro-Stories

SØREN KIERKEGAARD CLAIMS, AGAINST Hegel, the asymmetry and the elusiveness of the particular in importance of the universal, and does so through three main critiques.[1] First, Hegel argues that existence is subordinate to essence because the real always becomes rational, and the particular is necessarily then pushed to submit to and align with the universal. For Kierkegaard, on the other hand, existence cannot be subordinate to essence because essence is only conceptual—a gnoseological process of abstraction of the human mind—while what is real is the particular and individual existence. Second, Hegel develops his philosophy around a dialectical process between thesis, antithesis, and synthesis, where the particular, understood as difference, is considered only transitory, subsequently swallowed up by the final synthesis. Kierkegaardian dialectics is instead tensional and paradoxical (*aut . . . aut*), not synthetic like the Hegelian one (*et . . . et*), in which individuals remain in their singularity because they choose and are chosen between irreconcilable alternatives. Third, in the Hegelian system, necessity triumphs, as everything happens according to a rational order established by the absolute. It cannot be otherwise. Kierkegaard instead opposes existence as possibility to this mandatory, rational necessity. Individuals are not what they are prescribed to be from outside (heteronomy) but what they choose to be from inside (autonomy). Not the great history but the

1. Kierkegaard, *Fear and Trembling*, 15–35.

particular stories—the stories of individuals, the micro-stories—constitute true reality.

Europe, beyond some important traits inherited from Hegel and his rationalistic system, is today more Kierkegaardian than Hegelian. It has become even more so in recent decades when respect for differences has become the main criterion for verifying every system. In addition to this, monolithic and compact systems have become the object of radical and continuous critique.

The validation of the "particular" passes through local territories— the singular national territories with their own languages, histories, and traditions. European Adventism is not only divided theologically from an abstract, legitimate, but reductive perspective, it's originally diversified culturally from its various deep-rooted souls linked to particular territories. According to Edward Casey, in his insightful text on the modern understanding of space, determinant for peoples' identity is not "universal territory" (space), but rather the "particular territories" (places) they interact with.[2] Because places, adds French anthropologist Marc Augé, are always contaminated spaces, human-lived, and human-invaded spaces.[3] They are touched and irreversibly marked by human-specific stories and events. While "spaces" are uncontaminated and aseptic territories, "places" are territories touched and contaminated by what is human. This is why true religions must be necessarily contaminated, touched, and positively modified by the territories in which they come into contact, which affirms John Inge in his book *A Christian Theology of Place*.[4]

European Adventism inherited this diffuse attention to singular identities and cultural differences based on the validation of local territories. Two traits characterize European Adventism: its smallness and the heterogeneity and differentiation of this smallness. This allows us to outline a sociological rule, introduced in the second part of the eighteenth century by Ferdinand Tönnies.[5] The larger a human group, the more it tends to be culturally homogeneous (*gesellschaft*/society). The smaller a human group, the more it tends to preserve its cultural difference (*gemeinschaft*/community). The "particular," therefore, tends to break the symmetry of the system. In fact, life, if it is a particular life, always goes beyond the rules that

---

2. Casey, *Fate of Place*.
3. Augé, *No-Places*.
4. Inge, *Christian Theology of Place*.
5. Tönnies, *Gemeinschaft und Gesellschaft*.

Part I: Compulsions and Sublimations

try to regulate it. In this, it is essentially transgressive. No life, individual, or community is tautological. Life is always creative and configures itself as a particular, unique, and singular life.

European Adventism is very small numerically. The Inter-European Division (EUD), based in Bern, Switzerland, has 180,000 Adventists for 340 million people. Trans-European-Division (TED), based in Hertfordshire near London, England, has even fewer: 87,000 Adventists out of 205 million people. If we take, for example, the case of only two nations, Italy and France, we recognize the numerical fragility of European Adventism. In France, there are 11,000 Adventists for 68 million inhabitants. In Italy, there are 9,000 Adventists for more than 60 million inhabitants. The only educational institution in Italy is the Adventist School of Religion in Florence, where Italian pastors receive their theological and pastoral training.

In addition its reduced population, European Adventism is distinguished by another important fact: European Adventism is divided both linguistically and culturally. So, not only is the total number of members small, but that small number is further fragmented into various linguistic and cultural realities that interact relatively little and poorly. With fewer than 160–170 theology students across the division (EUD), we have seven Schools of Religion and two official division schools: Collonges (France) and Friedensau (Germany). For such a small population of students, this entails a significant financial burden.

Yet, even this seemingly negative fact embodies a view of life and history that distinguishes European culture and, consequently, European Adventism. This is the validation of local entities, of singular territories, of small communities, and "little stories" ("micro-stories"). At a cultural level, this attention to "small local realities" is manifested, for example, in a movement of historical thought, born in Italy in the 1970s and bearing the name "microhistory." Its best-known representative is historian Carlo Ginzburg, who has been professor at the "Scuola Normale" in Pisa, Harvard, Yale, Princeton, and UCLA. Ginzburg[6] presented his book *The Thread and the Traces* in 2015 at the Adventist University in Florence.

In contrast to great systems of analysis and interpretation of history, such as the Marxist or the structural-functionalist perspectives, which choose to consider the great trends and orientations of general human events, Ginzburg and his school of thought choose rather to consider very circumscribed geographical areas and human events. This allows a

---

6. Ginzburg, *Threads and Traces*.

meticulous and analytical reconstruction of the history of small local communities. It looks at events, characters, and anthropological attitudes that are inevitably lost in large-scale historical descriptions. General categories (state, social orders, economic systems, etc.) and conventional historical periods (Medieval, Modern, and Contemporary) tend to overlook, says Ginzburg, the pertinence of these particular and small human events. The major contributions made by this line of research are the ability to grasp elements of continuity and change hidden behind traditional social patterns. It also introduces new sources and methods offered, on the one hand, by the small details of minor biographies and, on the other hand, by specific attitudes and reactions to such behaviors, strategies, memories, beliefs, fears, and collective doubts.

"Microscopic" observation, conducted with particular procedures, shows things that from a larger perspective and with standard methodologies could not be seen. Some of these procedures are:

1) The Relevance of the Particular and the Individual

Microhistory acknowledges the historical value and dignity of the particular on its own. The particular doesn't need to be rescued by general historical categories or periods. This is because the *individual* embodies the anomalous fact, the emergence of the unexpected, the exception, and the cultural and historical asymmetry that has enormous value in bringing us back to concrete reality in human experience. The possibility of starting from or grasping individual perspectives, however, does not lead to historical skepticism. That is abhorred by micro-historians. Instead, every social, cultural, and economic *configuration* is the result of the interaction of countless individual strategies that give general trends another rhythm and flavor. At a religious level, this means that listening, of and to, singular individualities becomes mandatory. The system cannot disregard the relevance of the particular, with its voice and needs, as when individuals speak out their particular views on global orientations of a church-system.

2) The Constraint of Diverse Contexts

The focus on the particular and on the individual naturally gives rise to the question on how to consider heterogeneous contexts. Each of these can be traced back to the corresponding individual identity. So various contexts are linked to the variety of individuals. This, however, is not the main implication. What mainly marks the existence of differentiated contexts is the convergence of these various contexts in each individual identity. Individual identity is therefore influenced by various contexts. Everyone is then composite and plural. Plurality is not only outside but inside each identity. An identity does not belong to and doesn't exhaust its profile in connection to a single context. Differentiated contexts are also a reflection of heterogeneous and multilayered identities. It is as if everyone lives multiple realities. Historical actors are thus inscribed in contexts of different dimensions and levels, from religious to secular, from the national to that of their immediate territory. Therefore, there is no opposition between local and global history. At the religious level, this fact calls attention to the need of understanding multiple realities. One is not solely a member of a particular church. One simultaneously belongs to different cultural, political, or social groups with which religious belonging must be able to know and negotiate.

3) The Value of Paradoxes

"Microhistory" is wary of current uses of seriality, indexing, or cataloguing, which take into account only comparable homogeneities. Instead, it uses *anomalies* (traces, clues, exceptions, asymmetries, etc.) to shed light on otherwise conformity-based events. Through the *"atypical" and the "exceptional,"* the inconsistencies of reality and normative systems emerge. Then, within this context, strategic paths of historical actors are constructed. Their creativity, their ability to bargain and to transform, is thus highlighted, not the mere responsiveness and obedience to context, as functionalism had instead suggested. At a religious level, this implies that the discomfort of believers with theological and ecclesiastical models that are excessively monolithic and compact, which do not take into account the irregularity and exceptions in the life of faith, is not necessarily an anomaly but rather an asset that can help to correct or reorient the whole system. Faith paradoxes are not the problem but rather the pilot flame of a healthy religious wandering.

4) The Need for Reasonable Strategies

The concept of strategy, as used by microhistory, is very different from that associated with optimizing rationality. For microhistory, strategies are options within possibilities, driven by feelings, beliefs, and motivations. They are in themselves the characters of the project. The *processual* and *generative* character of historical contexts are constructed by interweaving partial visions, limited rationalities, provisional transactions, conflicts, and negotiations. From a functionalist perspective, these would normally be read only on the basis of their conclusive outcomes. In the same way, the analysis of the social categories (classes, corporations, the market, kinship) cannot be posited by adhering uncritically to one of their final representations; they must be reformulated by following the process of their construction. At a religious level, this implies that faith and existence remain united in a tensional way as much as consistency with flexibility, or conviction with reasonableness, in an open process of a flourishing faith.

5) The Value of Incompleteness, Partiality, and Distortions

Therefore, any kind of historical narrative, according to microhistory, is necessarily incomplete and partial. Gaps and distortions of documentation are part of the narrative. Micro-historical construction, however, is not incompatible with *proof* or with the *reality principle*. Every narrative is like a map that then has to be compared with the territory. As a map, it will have gaps and inaccuracies that will gradually be corrected by this very comparison with the real territory. Gaps and distortions are not problems in themselves but rather a resource and an opportunity to come nearer to human territory. At a religious level, this means that instruments (churches, institutions, the Bible) never become ends in themselves. The medium is not absolute but relative (relational); it retains its worth only in a continuous and honest comparison with the territory of life and history. Gaps and distortions are not obstacles but mediations and mediators for remaining attached to reality. In this sense, every belief system or faith community is healthy only when it acknowledges the inevitable and structural gaps and distortions of its own system. Every religious group is born already unilateral, incomplete, and distorted, even though this fact is invisible at the beginning because it is covered by the initial fervor, euphoria, and compact militancy.

These five characteristics listed by Carlo Ginzburg to construct "microhistories" are actually not created by him; he takes them from European culture. This is a culture attentive to the particular, and by virtue of this, distrusts monolithic, compact, totalizing, and excessively pragmatic and functional systems. Europe has had to learn this fact from its own history, with extreme pain.

Part I: Compulsions and Sublimations

Consequently, European Adventism, conditioned and shaped positively by this sensitivity to the particular and this focus on the exception, looks sometimes with surprise, sometimes with bewilderment, at the compact militancy of "mainline" Adventism. This "mainline" approach instead makes "universal" the reference category of its theology, its eschatology, even its administration. In fact, the "one rule for all" formula is as discouraging and alienating as the opposing "each with his own rule" formula.

This is what Seyla Benhabib means in her analysis of the work of three European thinkers—Hannah Arendt, Walter Benjamin, and Theodor Adorno—when she says that public and social administration is always arduous, demanding work, precisely because one cannot proceed by standard measures in the face of human groups, secular or religious, because of what she calls "the elusiveness of the particular."[7] Systems become functional and effective by standardizing persons and events. In this, they express an ambivalence—the ambivalence of efficiency and reification. There is thus always an excess of the particular over rules, of life over regulations, of persons over doctrines and ecclesiastical programs. Real life is always particular because, as Nobel price chemist and physicist Ilya Prigogine observes, particular life unfailingly remains incomparable, mysterious, and unavailable.[8]

---

7. Benhabib, "Elusiveness of the Particular," 34–60.
8. Prigogine, *End of Certainty*.

4

Complexity and Diasporic Identities

MILAN KUNDERA, THE CZECH-BORN and naturalized French writer, published his novel *The Unbearable Lightness of Being* in 1984.[1] In this book, he narrates the paradoxes of love between the main character, Tomas, and his fiancée, Tereza. The book does not just describe the paradoxical adventures of a young doctor who loves and betrays, works diligently and is libertine, preserves and innovates his own tradition. Italo Calvino, in his book *American Lessons*, takes it as an example of the true novel because, hiding behind the theme of "lightness," its true goal is to articulate a reflection "on the inescapable complexity of living."[2] It is a book about life, its heaviness, and the insurmountable difficulty of being able to reduce it to a sentence, a formula, or a synthetic theological or moral judgment. Complexity belongs to life as much as life belongs to complexity. Healthy identities are neither homogeneous nor compact because they try to interact and assimilate that complexity as it articulates and expands in real life.

The incorporation of that complexity changes identities by making them diasporic. Kundera's Tomas and Tereza have diasporic selves. A diasporic self, that Paul Ricœur calls "oneself as another,"[3] is neither a disper-

---

1. Kundera, *Unbearable Lightness of Being*.

2. Published in English under the title *Six Memos for the Next Millennium*. Calvino, *Six Memos*, 7–8.

3. Ricœur, *Oneself as Another*.

Part I: Compulsions and Sublimations

sive nor a cohesive self. A relational self maintains the positive tension of relationality at its center. The necessary existential unity and convergence of the various dimensions of our life are not glued in an irreversible synthesis but rather interact in a sort of internal communion that is intentional but not necessarily aware.[4] There is, then, for the diasporic self, a social communion marked by empathic actions toward others outside. It is also an internal communion marked by an empathic soul taking care and creating convergence of the various components of our inside self. The failure of the diasporic self in creating internal differentiation and convergence entails the emergence of pathological dispersion[5] (psychotic schizophrenia) and its opposite, pathological homogeneity (psychotic paranoia). The diasporic self is then a "kenotic self"—a self that has given up the illusion of full control over its own identity. Gayatri Spivak and Judith Butler maintain that the pretended sovereignty of the Westphalian State (modern state), as much as it presupposed and parallel anthropological correspondence, "the sovereign self," are both an illusion.[6]

Kundera's "Lightness of Being" can then be of two types. "Superficial lightness" is linked to being monolithic, either in living vices or virtues. The initial benefit of compactness turns out to be hell because neither nuances nor specificities, which are typical of true life, are really taken into account. Existence, secular or religious, is standardized. Instead, "paradoxical lightness" is rewarding in the long term, even though it initially appears as unbearable because it introduces in its own way a kind of opacity and resistance that typically are linked to people and events—and are irreducible to simple ethical forms or social schemes. Our pace here becomes immediately slower and demands humility. It even creates frustration because nuances, particularities, and unprevented events don't depend on our will but are naturally imposed on us as genuine components of human living. "Paradoxical lightness" teaches us to understand that life is relation, and that relation means learning to deal with diversity, with alternatives, with resistance, and even opposition without becoming anxious or escaping.

Paradoxical lightness, as much as the *holzwege* metaphor introduced in a previous chapter, reminds us that life, secular or spiritual, is made up of multiple and recurring existential paradoxes and juxtapositions that

---

4. Fodor, *Modularity of Mind*.
5. McWilliams, *Psychoanalytic Diagnosis*, 43–69.
6. Butler, *Who Sings the Nation-State?*

intersect and overlap in life and faith, without the possibility of arriving at a final synthesis. Complexity is an essential part of life at its best expression.

European culture, as Kundera reminds us in a small but dense book of essays called *The Art of the Novel*,[7] is neither homogeneous nor monolithic; it has complexity at its center by hosting two opposing souls within itself from the very beginning: a rationalistic soul based on linearity and clarity, and a narrative soul based on complexity and ambivalence.

Europeans, however, tend to consider only part of their own tradition: the rationalist and constructivist part. As Hannah Arendt reminds us, they have invested a lot in reason and will as main categories to know and to control reality.[8] And those who invest in reason and will tend to overlook complexity. In this sense, Europe has been continually tempted to perceive itself only as a dynamic and homogeneous culture based on a strong rationalist thrust going back to Descartes's *Cogito*. The dark side of dynamism is the homogenization of life or institution. There is an inversely proportional relationship of one to the other. The more we lose in complexity the more we gain in dynamism. The more dynamic one becomes, the more one glosses over and forgets complexity.

Europe has often fallen into the trap that has pushed it to overlook the complexity of its own identity. In fact, Europe will not shape itself as a culture of order and efficiency when it discovers a new epistemology, science, or politics, but rather when it detaches itself from "others," overlooking the life's structural complexities. "Others" should be understood not just as different populations but also as different species. This mechanism is a continuum in the history of modern Europe. Only when we detach ourselves from others and from the complexity that those lives introduce into reality do we become truly and finally efficient and dynamic. Byung-Chul Han reminds us that progress, whether cultural or social, has a hidden face, which is the exclusion of the "other."[9] By doing so, it also excludes complexity.

The presence of others always introduces an element of confusion, opacity, and disorder that prevents a perfect social order. And the same mechanism occurs at the level of church and theology. The clearer and more dynamic a church and its theology become, the more that church tends to gloss over and ignore the complexity of a faith experience.

---

7. Kundera, *Art of the Novel*.
8. Arendt, *Human Condition*, 248–320.
9. Han, *Espulsione dell'altro*.

Part I: Compulsions and Sublimations

Others always slow our pace and act as disturbing obstacles through the incomparable opacity of their mystery. In the narrative of modern man, this element is decidedly neglected, and the drive for an orderly future and growth is exclusively seen as a virtue. Instead, passion for an orderly and efficient world is the sign of a loss—an anthropological loss, the loss of the other. It is marked by structural ambiguity because, on the one hand, it has given rise to an incredible organizational and creative dynamism, the basis of Europe's progress. But on the other hand, there is a dark side. From the beginning, there has been minimization, discrediting, and finally, oppression and exploitation of other peoples. Paradoxically, it results in the attrition and alienation of its own project of civilization.

European epistemology, and the culture to which it gives birth, could also be understood as essentially an anthropological problem. The detachment and estrangement from other peoples, notably from the Global South, represents the ambivalent primordial node and the cultural "thermometer" of European culture. Anomaly is therefore present from the beginning in its foundations, in the European DNA. In 1580, Michel de Montaigne had already said that Europe was being born as a new world under the sign of a new rationality and efficiency, but with two basic structural anomalies. In the "Apology of Raimond Sebond," the philosopher describes a Europe breaking away from other peoples, whom it contemptuously calls uncivilized and primitive.[10] But Europe was also breaking away from nature (that is, from other species), to create wealth and progress by manipulating them. Montaigne saw not only the correlation of these two phenomena, "racism" and "speciesism," but managed to glimpse, in the birth of Europe, the seed of its own perversion and self-destruction.

The merit of Kundera and the texts cited above remind us that Europe, despite this historical tendency toward homogenizing dynamism, has, in fact, a dual soul. If Descartes represents the "soul of ideation" ("clear and distinct ideas"), later to become clarity of social and political action, then the "soul of complexity," according to Kundera, manifests itself mainly in the modern novel. The prototype of the modern novel, after Kundera, is Miguel de Cervantes' *Don Quixote*. So, what distinguishes this seventeenth-century story as insightful into this other European soul?

In the first chapter of Kundera's *The Art of the Novel*, "The Depreciated Legacy of Cervantes," Kundera summarizes the profile of this second European soul, which is generally overlooked but has always been present

---

10. Montaigne, *Saggi*, 489–683; chapter 12 of the second book.

and is incarnated in the modern European novel. This second soul tempers the euphoria and mysticism of European visionaries fascinated by a culture of scientific and social progress. This second soul represents sensitivity, listening, and the perception of the indelible complexity of life that often hides behind the "lightness of being." In fact, Kundera adds, in the novel there is not a single protagonist but a collection of figures and characters that can hardly be framed into a single paradigm. The plot of the novel is always made up of multilinear and polyvalent entrances and exits that the narrator only tries to describe and join, without claiming to arrive at a synthetic truth. In the novel, the plot is always fluid; what precedes does not mechanically determine what follows. A new datum, an unexpected gesture, an unplanned event emerges continuously and directs everything in an unexpected path. A final synthesis is impossible. Thus, doubt, multiplicity, fragmentation, and surprise remain.

Kundera has done nothing more than to "photograph" the complexity of life and history that Europe has, with difficulty, integrated into its DNA. So, compared with the United States, Europe appears as a slow continent, sometimes bent over its own past with a melancholic, even cynical, and certainly more tragic soul. But what is seen as a handicap in the face of American efficiency and dynamism is in reality an anthropological and cultural richness that Europe itself must learn to appreciate and share in today's necessary and difficult multicultural dialogue.

European Adventist theology, the academic as much as the implicit theology of the grassroots communities, has absorbed this sensitivity to the complexity of life and faith. If European Adventism does not grow as much as world Adventism, it is certainly not because of laziness or indolence. It is primarily because of this holzwege-complexity that neither Adventist institution nor our Adventist mission should ever forget.

European Adventism, despite appearances, does not have that semi-Pelagian soul that has tormented world Adventism since its inception. For many, this is a drift, a flaw. But in the overall picture of global Adventism, this fact represents an asset. As such, it stands as a resource to be drawn upon to give greater substance, value, and robustness to Adventist identity worldwide.

5

The Ambivalence of Militancy

MILITANCY IS AN ESSENTIAL ingredient for the birth and growth of a religious experience, whether individual or corporate. Without militancy, the component giving consistency and stability to a faith experience would be missing. At a theoretical level, militancy entails beliefs and values; at a more practical level, it involves consistency and discipline. Yet, militancy, when it stands alone, not only fails to ensure healthy growth but also runs the risk of deforming our identity. For this reason, militancy must necessarily be accompanied by healthy reflection, as Amos Oz reminds us in his book *How to Cure a Fanatic*.[1] But militancy does not like reflection; it only likes "reflection" that confirms, not contradicts.

True reflection is not that which confirms militancy but rather that which shakes it—shakes it with troubling questions. If reflection is not disturbing, it is not reflection at all. This is why Max Weber described the true political leader as one who can hold, or learn how to hold, the indelible tension between militancy and reflection—between, what he called, "charisma and responsibility."[2] Here, responsibility means the ability to reflect with enthusiasm on what we do. It involves the capacity of evaluating not only one's convictions but also to critically assess the resulting effects of our

---

1. Oz, *How to Cure a Fanatic*, 16.
2. Weber, *Politik als Beruf*, 23.

The Ambivalence of Militancy

actions and strategies. This especially includes unintended consequences that conviction often minimizes or tends not to see.

If Adventism tends to be an ethical theology, one of the main categories at play—both ethical and theological—will necessarily be militancy. Indeed, mainline Adventism overwhelmingly prioritizes the figure of a militant believer. Not only does it fail to see other profiles as equally worthy, but, more importantly, it fails to perceive the anomalies in its own model. As happens with models that have become ideological, discomforts and anomalies are attributed to the failure in applying more consistently defended models. People don't see that anomalies can be created by the presupposed ideal model itself. So, people try to correct this with an updated form of the same model that has caused those same anomalies.

Adventism, paradoxically, did not invent the model of a militant ethics; it inherited it from modernity itself. Wolfhart Pannenberg reminds us of this when he says that, from the typical religious foundation of pre-modern ethics, modernity replaces it with an ethics detached from God.[3] We might have expected the decay of ethics in modernity, but instead, Pannenberg continues, we find its reinforcement through two paradoxes.

First, ethics do not decay but are reinforced. Second, the classical subordination of ethics to dogmatics is replaced by the subordination of dogmatics to ethics. That is, only those theological statements that have a practical ethical effect will be validated. The testing ground of theology and its validity is given now by ethics. In this sense, all contemporary theology is an ethical theology. But at the same time, ethical theology implicitly secularizes faith, because the validating element becomes a nontheological element: ethical practice. The mystical-spiritual dimension that hitherto characterized a faith experience then tends to disappear. Kierkegaard will react against this typical ethical-modern trend by trying to safeguard the specific spiritual dimension of religion from the invasiveness of ethics and its excessive practical rationality. The essence of religion, according to Kierkegaard, always lies beyond the ethical dimension.[4]

Militants, by virtue of their obsession with application at the expense of reflection, introduce a strong element of practical rationality, even when railing against speculative rationality. Adventism has merely adopted this distinctive feature of modern and contemporary Christianity by uniquely giving it a different justification. The experience of faith requires and

3. Pannenberg, *Grundlagen der Ethik*, 2–17.
4. Kierkegaard, *Fear and Trembling*, 4–15.

PART I: COMPULSIONS AND SUBLIMATIONS

demands a specific mark to act correctly and consistently. So, Adventism creates a perfectly practical rationalism that tends to erase not only reflection but anything else that contradicts the linearity of militancy.

For mainline Adventism, therefore, only the one who acts—with determination and avoiding distraction—is a consistent believer. To this, performative ethics of immediate action, typical of radical militancy, corresponds a flat anthropology of a linear and transparent identity. The complexity of individuals and their actions are completely ignored here. As Chinese Philosopher Li Zehou reminds us, the militant has a subjectivity that is too linear.[5] The militant finds completely foreign what Li Zehou calls "subjectality," understood as a complex subjectivity built up in a healthy relation with the external world on the basis of a plurality of dimensions of the self.

For the militant, any interruption of the desired action is necessarily perverse because it diverts us from the goal. He who knows and does not act is necessarily inconsistent because the knowledge possessed does not lead to concrete action. Adventist ethics has always been shaped by this strong prescriptive component. Current Adventism, instead of mitigating this trend, is instead reinforcing and radicalizing it with its typical missiological and eschatological urgency.

Such a strongly prescriptive ethics presupposes two conditions: first, that the historical context be transparent; second, precisely because it is so clear, there is then only one possible action to follow without delay. This prescriptive ethics has not faded with time but has paradoxically strengthened.

Today, the Adventist prescriptive ethics has become more radical for various reasons. Let's just mention two of them. First, because of what is perceived as evangelistic urgency, one cannot convince "the world" with a confusing and complex message. So, to evangelize, the gospel must be reduced to clear and convincing slogans. Both ethical and theological complexity tends to be worn down by this obsession with a warped version of witness. Second, because of administrative homogeneity, Adventism stubbornly wants to reinforce a greater efficiency. Unity is conceived as uniformity. While this unity was promoted only at a theological level in the past, current Adventism is now obsessed with administrative homogeneity as well. A true church cannot indulge in the luxury of hesitancy or uncertainty, much less doubt or repentance. Clear and unambiguous decisions are marks and proofs of true coherence and militancy.

---

5. Zehou, *Humanist Ethics*, 11–21.

European Adventism breaks away from this model, not because it considers it unnecessary but simply because it considers it insufficient. Instead, European Adventism has always favored an "elective" ethics instead of the typical "prescriptive" ethic of mainline Adventism. This elective ethics presupposes two specific conditions.

First, the complexity of the situation; it is not always possible to know what to do because the situation has become complex from both a religious and human perspective. European culture is not only complex but Europeans are generally aware of this complexity and therefore wary of reductive slogans. Moreover, this attention to religious complexity is not new. It belongs to the ethics of the prophets, as opposed to the ethics of the Torah, which appears decidedly more compact and almost dualistic in reference to the conceptions of virtue and errors (Deut 28).

Second, there is no single option for one's action. Therefore, before I can act, I must necessarily understand the meaning of these various options available. In European Adventism, prescriptive ethics has been replaced with reflective ethics that tries to understand before acting. The typical Adventist ethics of obedience is then substituted by a kind of, what we could call, "wisdom ethics." How could we apply a principle if the contexts are not clear and we don't understand what present circumstances demand from us?

Seen from this perspective, ethics requires and introduces a new anthropology. Indeed, ethics is not just about the action but also about ethical agents—persons and their complexity—behind those actions. Militant ethics tends to focus on an action's effectiveness while engulfing the person behind it. Reflective ethics instead takes charge of the person and the multilayer condition a person always presupposes, including feelings and non-rationalistic elements.

At this level, European Adventism implicitly suggests new criteria for action. One of these new criteria is "orthopathy." Biblical beliefs (orthodoxy) and consistent, disciplined behavior (orthopraxy) are no longer sufficient. A third register is needed that takes into account the health and balance of the believer as a person. Orthopathy is the register of a healthy interiority of one's attitudes and feelings. Believers "who know" and "who act" could be worn out, anxious, and related to their community in the same unilateral and anomalous way.

This is what psychoanalyst Christopher Bollas describes in his book *Meaning and Melancholia*.[6] He reminds us that militancy without reflection

---

6. Bollas, *Meaning and Melancholia*, 4–21.

hides a self that is worn out, suffering, and also divided. This is because, in the face of militancy's own internal suffering, it is incapable of stopping for self-care. It therefore proceeds by compulsion. Compulsion makes militants appear even more performative—without realizing that such militancy is a compensation mechanism for concealment and dissembling. Militants often cannot read themselves or their own suffering and misery. They have unfortunately internalized a pattern of action that saves and condemns them at the same time. It saves because it makes them feel useful and redeems them from insignificance and anonymity. Yet, it perpetuates their discomfort and existential asymmetry.

Today's militancy has unfortunately become the polite and decent word that describes worn-out and suffering believers who nevertheless cannot do without the reassurance and comfort of their compulsive rituals. This becomes a kind of addiction. Even when those actions, tasks, and goals are unnecessary, militants must ritualistically perform them in order not to feel lost in their own suffering, which they do not want to see. This artificial net of goals, actions, and strategies that compulsive militants perceive as mandatory for themselves and their own spiritual balance, because they have no empathy at all, they then try to impose as mandatory for others. The proof of others' sincerity is that they do as I do and think, say militants to themselves.

Religious militants then become kinds of "serial compulsive pragmatics." When such a profile is at the top of the decision-making power of an institution or community, the same model is transferred to the whole community. This is why Christopher Bollas speaks of the "manic" tendency of pragmatism in today's performance societies, of which militant believers are merely an extension. Militancy is a modern phenomenon. It does not belong to the biblical record, despite continuing intentions to ground it in Scripture. But this compulsion to act is even more dangerous because it is implemented as a mechanism for hiding one's own suffering and attrition. In many ways, pressed by the apocalyptic urgency, today's Adventism tends not only to become compulsive but, unfortunately, also manic in its ethics and eschatology. This is why European Adventism, for the reasons briefly described above, is not a threat but rather part of the solution for both Adventist ethics and, paradoxically, for a renewed concept of witness and evangelism.

6

The Challenge of Bottom-Up Ethics

NOBODY DOUBTS THAT ETHICS represents an important human and religious dimension in which to verify not only the coherence between what we say and what we do but, particularly, the anthropological health and richness of the ethical agent, which should always be presupposed behind each action. In other words, ethics is not only about what we do but also about what we are, as Kwame Anthony Appiah from Princeton University reminds us in his book *The Ethics of Identity*.[1] For this reason, it's not enough to assess the consistency of the prescriptive element, typical of ethics, and the parallel obedience to it, typical of a morally reliable individual. When the "prescriptive element" becomes dysfunctional to action, it is necessary to rediscover the regenerating power or "descriptive dimension" of ethics, as described by Arthur Schopenhauer in the fourth and last part of his book *The World as Will and Representation*.[2] "Ethical description" can save a dysfunctional "prescriptive ethics." Descriptive ethics is in essence a bottom-up ethics.

Adventism has always considered descriptive ethics with suspicion because it is not prescriptive enough. But when the prescriptive component of ethics not only doesn't promote action but paralyzes it, we should then turn to see and verify whether the defended prescription does or does not correspond to the nature of persons or communities involved in that

1. Appiah, *Ethics of Identity*, 12–22.
2. Schopenhauer, *World as Will*, 53–54.

historical moment. That is precisely the challenge of a bottom-up ethics. It is fundamentally ethical, not by what prescribes the norm but by what makes human action possible. And sometimes, to make possible an action is not "prescription" but "description."

From its inception, Adventism has embraced a theology that has privileged ethics. All other load-bearing categories of Adventism—the Sabbath, second coming, anthropology, etc.—have been reworked, put into perspective, and refined by this ethical sensibility. It probably happened for several reasons.

The first is an understandable reaction to the major Protestant and evangelical churches in their efforts to disentangle themselves from Catholic collaborationism regarding salvation. Protestantism places ethics in an important though secondary dimension in believers' experience, detaching it from salvation itself, which happens only by God's grace. Adventism had the insight to understand that, while safeguarding the exclusivity of God's grace in the order of salvation, ethics is not so foreign to the salvific experience understood as a process. Adventism then paid particular attention in how to connect ethics with salvation by trying to avoid the overidentification of both, as does Catholicism, but also their over-separation, as happens in Protestantism.

The second reason was contextual—nineteenth-century "Puritan" America. This strongly pragmatic and moral context heavily conditioned the Adventist profile, which was born in this period and which, despite the explicit efforts to demarcate itself from that context, was nevertheless heavily conditioned by it.

Therefore, as opposed to an optimistic and spiritualizing tendency, Adventists played the sanctification card. The salvific process is thus incomplete if the "justification of the sinner" is not joined by the "transformation of the sinner." But as often happens in history (and particularly the history of Adventism), over time, the solution becomes part of the problem. The sanctification that was meant to complete the salvation process ends up deforming it. Instead of being an ally, sanctification becomes a hindrance to believers' flourishing. The resulting salvation is then one-sided and overly predictable. The Adventist version of the gospel does not save believers but tends to congeal and stiffen them into being more distrustful, compulsive, and cynical about life and others.

Adventism lacks, as indeed do all religious communities, a serious effort in differential diagnosis. Religions tend to believe that promoting spirituality is enough to contrast materialism, secularism, and other sorts of anthropological anomalies and dysfunctions. However, religious anomalies are not only by default but also by excess. While Adventism is more attentive to the former, it is very naive with respect to the latter. It is important to consider, following an "ethics of paradox," that not only vices but also virtues often become part of the problem. People's lives are often ruined not by vices but by unmonitored virtues. And the same paradox can be found beyond ethics in belief systems as well. Doctrinal errors aren't the only way to warp the path of faith; unmonitored biblical truths can also distort it. Often, people's spiritual experience isn't compromised by theological errors but rather by biblical truths that have become schematic and excessively one-sided. Ethics, as much as belief, is not only a matter of correct ingredients but also a matter of proportions, relations, balances, rhythm, and wisdom.

Adventism is challenged today not by exogenous elements (Catholicism, materialism, secularism, etc.) but rather by endogenous elements (Bible, prophecies, tradition, etc.). We don't succeed in assembling positively in a life-promoting soil mostly because we have stopped being relational. Only a constant and trusting relation with external realities, persons, groups, or events give the measure of life's true rhythm, proportion, and timing. Adventism is warped less by wrong things than by biblical truths that have paradoxically become an iron cage, inhibiting the Spirit, life, and common sense. This happens through excessive zeal, compact conviction, and blind militancy. These are hallmarks of reductive and pragmatic religiosity.

It is often difficult to know whether we have become religiously schematic because we are not truly relational, or whether we are not relational because we have a schematic and pragmatic ethos. Both things are eventually true. This reductive attitude, which tends to consider persons and events, is the cause and consequence of our inability to dialogue. Those who are excessively pragmatic and want to achieve results immediately cannot waste time in dialogue. It forces them not only to slow down their path of "progress," and possibly to even revise it, but more fundamentally, it is this unwillingness to dialogue that drives believers into a convinced but one-sided militancy. The problem is even broader because it also affects how one reads the Bible. The pragmatic spirit sees only what it needs to see in the Bible. It completely loses sight of its tensions, paradoxes, and alternatives. Our reductive ethics corresponds to our reductive hermeneutics. They go hand in hand.

Part I: Compulsions and Sublimations

In contrast, European Adventism, which is slower and numerically negligible, has always had a greater respect for human dialogue and thus for the plurality of meanings within the Bible. This sensibility, attentive to dialogue and complexity, which some consider a defect, makes European Adventism more alert and connected with reality. The typical "top down" ethics of sanctification puts the yardstick outside believers (in God, the Bible, or the church). European Adventism, on the other hand, embodies a "bottom up" ethics, which puts the starting point in believers themselves. Even to mention this possibility seems and sounds sacrilege to mainline Adventism.

The ethics of sanctification is necessary but insufficient because of its constant call to be like someone else (Paul, Jesus, etc.). It asks us to be what we are not yet and what we could be. But it also easily falls into denial of believers and what believers are by virtue of the gifts God has given everybody.

A "bottom up" ethics, cultivated across the board by European Adventism, is one that doesn't deny sanctification but nevertheless puts it in context with what we might call an ethics of "flourishing." Massimo Recalcati, a well-known Lacanian psychoanalyst, in one of his presentations in our Adventist School of Theology in Florence, reminded us that an ethics of "flourishing" (which he calls an "ethics of desire") is where believers *count*.[3] An individual's words, questions, gifts, sensitivities, rhythms, doubts, and slowness all count. We are not called to be like the apostle Paul or one of our pioneers, we are simply called to be ourselves. Each of us must be faithful to that gift, that character, that calling God has placed in our identities as unique and peculiar human beings.

It is what Spinoza called "conatus," that is, persevering in our own being, trying to be *ourselves*.[4] In a provocative way, Lacan, at the end of the seventh seminar, articulates in the following dictum:

> The only thing one can be guilty of is giving ground relative to one's desire.[5]

In this ethics of "flourishing," believers are called to make a case for what they are before God. Indeed, God demands it. To God's project, believers present their own perceptions and responses and their own version

---

3. Recalcati, *Elogio dell'inconscio*.
4. Spinoza, *Ethics*, 75.
5. Lacan, *Ethics of Psychoanalysis*, Seminar VII, 395.

of that project, being certain that God himself is the guarantor of this possibility and tension that necessarily emerges in this dialogue. If believers, therefore, are called to assert their own being before God, even more should they do so before Adventism, especially institutional Adventism. Indeed, true Adventism, like the true God, will be able to listen to and seriously consider the personal perception of each believer.

European Adventism is, in this respect, more Spinozian and also more Lacanian than Whitean. And this should not be imputed as a fault because of the ethics of one's own "flourishing." Though a minority in the face of the massive ethics of sanctification, it is nevertheless a model we find in the Bible itself. For example, in Ps 1:3,

> It will be like a tree planted along waterways,
> which will bear fruit in its own time
> And its leaves will never fall;
> it will succeed in all its works.

The tree reaches its life goal, not when it avoids sin but when it communicates life through its budding, its flowering, and its fruit. Flowering is a typical bottom-up model. The tree brings to fruition what it is. It is called to be itself. Every fruit, like every life, is a miracle—that is, a transgression. True life, like true love, is always transgressive because it knows how to go beyond what is logical, what is convenient, what others expect, what seems possible. So is the life-giving, incommensurate, over-the-top love of a father for a handicapped child, of a doctor for an irreversibly compromised life, of a teacher for a failing student.

This love would be impossible if we Christians clung only to the model of sanctification, of transformation, of dynamic movement. Taking up one's territory, taking root, knowing how to remain still, is a condition for flourishing (see Ps 46:10). The stillness of the tree, like the stillness of a life, has its own dignity, its own value. Healthy faith must recognize and appreciate this. Indeed, it is the antidote that this psalm proposes against a compulsive faith, obsessed with goals, results, and change.

At this point, the church model also changes. The goal of a faith community can no longer be the all-out walk—the mad rush toward seemingly religious but mechanically and artificially updated goals at the cost of detaching ourselves from everyone and everything. Believers' goal and purpose is to slow down the pace to be more with others in our community but also with others outside it. A "tree" does not belong only to a particular species but to the whole forest. This metaphor proposes a new model of living—and living together. It proposes a model of balance. Balance between the roots pointing to the earth and the branches pointing to the heavens. Balance between the leaves that highlight its own strength and exuberance and the fruit that is for others, never for the tree itself. Through its own fruit, the tree says, "The best of me is not meant for me but for others." The blossoming also becomes a noble way of witnessing where, without words, the tree offers the best of itself, its fruit, to those passing by. This is the anthropology presupposed by a bottom-up ethics.

7

Against Rectitude

"Rectitude" (righteousness) is an important religious and human value, but it's not absolute. No virtue is absolute. Vices and, paradoxically, also virtues can warp life and prevent us from doing what circumstances and God require of us. This happens when one ceases to monitor and direct them toward the promotion and flourishing of one's own life and the lives of others.

The overestimation of "rectitude" derives in part from overlooking persons as incarnate beings and from the abandonment of the body as regulator of anthropology and ethics. The theorical and practical predominance of the ideal over the material has led our current societies and communities to the negation of corporeal and incarnated existences. Secularization has not essentially changed this situation but simply has maintained it with scientific, social, and cultural arguments, derived no more from religion than from what Charles Taylor calls the "immanent frame."[1] In fact, Thomas Fuchs, Karl Jaspers professor of philosophy and psychiatry at Heidelberg University in Germany, establishes a worrying asymmetry between what he calls the "cyclical time" of the body and the "linear time" of modern institutions, which foster and promote psychological and bodily weariness and dissatisfaction.[2] The solution should not be to increase the pressure on

---

1. Taylor, *Secular Age*, 539–93.
2. Fuchs, "Cyclical Time."

persons through an increased refinement of ideals but rather the resizing of the hypertrophic profile of ideals, norms, and human and religious models.

But mainline Adventism has elevated rectitude to an absolute value, particularly in this end-time period, overlooking an important difference, as Hans LaRondelle used to say, between a legitimate aspiration to "perfection" and the obsession with "perfectionism."[3] While "perfection" remains relational to other synchronic virtues, "perfectionism" doesn't. "Perfectionism" is a self-referential attitude. Adventist perfectionism unilaterally starts from a well-known phrase by Ellen G. White in the book *Education*:

> The greatest want of the world is the want of men [and women] who will not be bought or sold, men [and women] who in their inmost souls are true and honest, men [and women] who do not fear to call sin by its right name, men [and women] whose conscience is as true to duty as the needle to the pole, men [and women] who will stand for the right though the heavens fall.[4]

An "ethics of rectitude," as expressed in this quotation, creates consistent and reliable believers from the standpoint of this expressed norm, but not necessarily from the standpoint of what circumstances require of us. Attention to circumstances, thus the very necessary connection with reality, is seen from this perspective as a useless, if not downright dangerous, exercise. Rectitude can easily become a self-referential exercise in which individuals obey only the internal forum of their own consciences. We should remember that, in our own conscience, we only have a subjective perception of God's commandment, not the direct commandment of God himself. We must not forget that external reality always serves as the true testing ground and verification of our moral actions and convictions. To construct a morality, a way of believing, a spirituality, only from an abstract ethical perspective, based on uniquely internal coherence, is short-sighted, limited, and counterproductive.

European Adventism has always been wary of this "ethics of rectitude," not because it fails to perceive its value but rather because it sees its limitations and one-sidedness. Instead, European Adventism embraces what we might call an "ethics of paradox," believing that dialogue with external realities (circumstances or people) is not only necessary but decisive. Only in connection with reality can a virtue or belief highlight its true value, goodness, and relevance.

3. LaRondelle, *Perfection and Perfectionism*.
4. White, *Education*, 57.

Connection with reality forces us into two important, though demanding and not always immediate, exercises. First, in ethical deliberation, not one single element can be taken into account (our conscience). Moral choice is complex precisely because of the plurality of heterogeneous and asymmetrical elements. We must take them all into account and learn to keep them in tension. Ethical choice cannot aim only at overcoming or erasing decision-making tension. Sometimes, the opposite is true. Ethical responsibility aims at *maintaining* that tension, which is a sign of life's complexities.

The second exercise is realizing that these "other elements," in relation to one's own consciousness, are not contour elements; they actually modify one's own consciousness and force it to compromise. Compromise is not a bad word. There are negative compromises, but there exist also positive ones. While the English language has a unique word for both types, the French language has two different words that express this difference. *Compromis* is the positive attitude of adapting and being flexible in some of our own prerogatives in order to reach the other. *Compromission* means instead giving up some of our essential convictions moved by a practical interest or advantage. Taken in a positive sense, compromise is then the commitment to seriously consider external reality as God's voice beyond our convictions, which are important but not absolute. God doesn't speak only to our conscience. He also speaks to us through what is outside us. The idealization of a pure and coherent consciousness thus appears to this "ethics of paradox" as a moral compulsion—a too linear ethical decision. It depends on an abstract, programmatic mechanism that refuses to reflect on the true meaning of one's action and limits itself to seek purely mechanical results, starting only from convictions.

This is what feminist philosopher Adriana Cavarero, from the University of Verona, reminded us during her visit to our Adventist School of Religion at *Villa Aurora-Florence* in presenting her book *Inclinations: A Critique of Rectitude*.[5] Cavarero reminded us that a one-sided attention and care for righteousness can become an obsession that deforms us. Human existence always presents itself with some opacity, with some curvatures ("inclinations"), which must not only be respected but also safeguarded. True morality is not human formatting according to some abstract model but listening to our humanity, linked to a respect for some of our most essential inclinations. Virtue has a double way of existing. It must change

---

5. Cavarero, *Inclinations*.

PART I: COMPULSIONS AND SUBLIMATIONS

reality by affecting it, but it also must be changed by the indelible curvatures of that surrounding reality. Sometimes a crooked reality is truer than an obsessively linear and straight virtue.

The one-sided aspiration for righteousness, from an ethical orientation, has now become a psychological attitude that Christopher Bollas calls, "normopathy."[6] Normopathy is that psychic dysfunction that forces us into formal righteousness (normality), which brackets the complexity of our deep self and external reality. Our living space can appear organized and ordered only when we shrink and detach it from the most typical and characterizing areas of our humanity. Humanity, in its truth and reality, is always curved and tilted. It is never "normal" nor "normalizable." In her book *Queer Theology*, Linn Marie Tonstad describes this legitimate curvature at the level of gender ("queer") and defends the curvature ("queerness").[7]

Life has an intrinsic structural opacity that resists our attempts to clear it up. In this, Tonstad is a courageous thinker for at least three reasons. First, because she doesn't escape but rather faces the human territory as it is without any theological or cultural sublimation. At least she tries. Second, in facing this human territory, she doesn't give up her faith. She explores it as a theologian—not as ecclesiocentric, but as a peripatetic theologian who walks and does theology in the streets and crossroads of current life, where every true theologian should be. That's where wisdom walks and calls (see Prov 8:1–3). Third, she is not afraid of contaminating theology if that means remaining faithful to the earth, to humanity, to the body. Relevant theology is always a "contaminated" theology. Purist theology is a de facto contradiction. Contamination is the true mark of theology's nobility and strength. It's what incarnation is all about. Tonstad's theology is thoroughly incarnated, bodily theology.

Let's now briefly describe why, after a European Adventist "ethics of paradox," humanity is necessarily "curved" and "queer." Then we'll consider why, as Cavarero, Bollas, and Tonstad have stated, a unilateral theology or "ethics of rectitude" compromises human and spiritual growth instead of promoting it.

---

6. Bollas, *Meaning and Melancholia*, 41–57.
7. Tonstad, *Queer Theology*.

1. EVERY REAL THING IS FACTUALLY "QUEER"

Over time, the word "queer" has gone through various definitions. We can discard the meaning of "queer" as oddity and choose instead that of asymmetry, surplus, and contingency.

- *Asymmetry* because the "queer" category claims validity for the *exception*, that which is under or over the norm, simply because the norm—any norm—is an ambivalent reality. It introduces order but also arbitrariness and exclusion.
- *Surplus* because "queer" is somewhat synonymous with excess, of an unexpected addition—the refreshing gift of unmerited flourishing.
- *Contingency* because "queer" doesn't obey the law of what is fixed, structurally necessary, or predetermined. Queer is the thing that couldn't be. It's not foreseen or planned but is, nevertheless. Queer is a temporally fragile event that dares to exist. It embodies the courage to be. When we consider these main characteristics of what "queer" can mean, we then perceive a surprising and strong parallelism with real life. True life manifests itself in the main stages of our existence as an asymmetric, excessive, and contingent event. Theology can't avoid becoming "queer" because it cannot afford to be detached from real life.

2. THE ASYMMETRIES OF A "QUEER" LIFE ARE NOT NECESSARILY PATHOLOGICAL

According to Michel Foucault, we live in a paradoxical historical season. On one side, it's a time of unlimited freedom. Conversely, there has never existed such a repressive society. Ours is a "panopticon society," characterized by repressing and ordering instances, paradoxically more implicit than explicit, and coming from below rather than above. While in pre-modern times, the order was static and independent of human intervention, in contemporary societies, the strong normative impulse is dynamic and man-made. It is particularly impregnated, as James Hillman notes,[8] with a strong tendency to pathologize the normal asymmetries of life, simply because these are not functional to the efficiency and goal-oriented perspective of our productive societies. In trying to make straight what is normally queer,

---

8. Hillman, *Re-Visioning Psychology*, 55–112.

functional societies use theology, religion, ethics, and medicine as their best and presumed-infallible allies. The asymmetries of queerness are not pathological; they could be the best expression of a true life—a life that is slow and vulnerable.

In this sense, European Adventism has tried to correct, or at least temper, the typical Pelagian soul of mainline Adventism, which is obsessed with rectitude. For the same reason, Martin Luther's idea of "simultaneously justified and sinner" (*simul peccator, simul iustus*) appears to mainline Adventism as a contradictory theological formula. But European Adventism sees it instead as a visionary and precious anthropological formulation of the complexity of life and salvation.

8

The Trap of Theological Universalism

It is currently believed that the value of a faith and a church lies in its universalism. If something is not valid for everyone, then that thing, or so it is thought, has no value at all. If, on the other hand, it is valid for everyone, then its validity would be guaranteed immediately. The problem with this conception of universalism easily leads us to an obsession with unity that becomes the standardization and homogenization of belief and faith. Moreover, by increasing rigidity, it does not allow us to grasp and live in the tension that true faith implies, which is a tension between the universal and the particular. Although the universalism of faith is true, it becomes false when it detaches itself and rejects this tensional dialogue with the particular. True dialogue between universalism and the particular does not take place when the universal organizes and normalizes the particular. When that happens, it ends up engulfing and neutralizing life and faith. True dialogue occurs when the universal allows itself to be countered and modified by the particular. It can then resize and reconfigure itself differently, starting from the protests and demands of the particular.

Misguided and misinformed identities believe that their strength lies in their universalism. Universal identities are in fact weak, not only because they are abstract but particularly because they are rigid, unable to deal with the unexpected and unprogrammed. This is what Yascha Mounk calls the

Part I: Compulsions and Sublimations

"Identity Trap."[1] The more people want long-standing security, the more they find refuge in the universal, ignoring that the universal is capable only of offering short-term security that is immediately challenged by the typical contingencies of real life. For the same reason, Daron Acemoglu and James A. Robinson, in their book *Why Nations Fail*, describe the damaging effect of abstract universalism, typical of what they call "extractive institutions,"[2] as opposed to "inclusive institutions" characterized by flexibility and adaptability.

When universalism becomes standard and no longer dialogues with the particular, it then ceases to be humane and becomes outright idolatry. This is Kierkegaard's radical critique of Hegel's rational and systemic universalism,[3] which Hegel encapsulated in the phrase "everything real is rational and everything rational is real."[4] But for Kierkegaard, truth is not in the universal but in the particular, not in categories but in exceptions.[5] The particular, in fact, always manifests itself in an exception that we all struggle to perceive and recognize in life. "Man," as a universal category, is not real—only a particular man, called specifically Carlo, Mario, or Alessandra.

Adventism, at present, seems to have lost the sense of the particular and seems to have capitulated to an abstract doctrinal universalism. The feelings and emotions of people, in their hesitations, vicissitudes, and vulnerability, do not matter much, as with the prophet Jonah in Nineveh. They are anomalies and asymmetries to be overcome as quickly as possible in the face of a universal, eschatological truth that demands clarity, compactness, and militancy. And right there—where obsession with the universal is accompanied by an ironclad pact with clarity, compactness, and militancy—is no place for human specificity. And if there is no humanity, there is no truth. And if human–truth is absent, there is no God either. Adventism, in the name of God and continually invoking his name, seems to be headed toward an idolatrous universalism. It does so not because what it says is false but rather because it says only part of the truth and is silent about that which guarantees a healthy manifestation of all truth, which certainly includes attention to the particular.

1. Mounk, *Identity Trap*, 10–25.
2. Acemoglu, *Why Nations Fail*, 34–53.
3. Kierkegaard, *Fear and Trembling*.
4. Hegel, *Elements of the Philosophy*, 20.
5. Kierkegaard, *Sickness unto Death*.

The Trap of Theological Universalism

Within this abstract Adventist universalism paradigm, everyone in the community must believe and do the same things, no matter where they are and to which culture they belong. This endogenous universalism then finds its natural extension in its parallel exogenous universalism. The only way to be acknowledged as full persons is for people to become Adventist, if not in fact, then at least in the fundamental traits of their humanity, which are necessarily Adventist. Adventist missiology is tainted by this false universalism that demands all believe the same way and in the same things—first, for those who are outside, but even more for those who are inside or have decided to come in.

But atypical European Adventism, the prodigal son of mainline Adventism, has reached a different conclusion. It believes in the foundational value of the particular and, consequently, spontaneously distrusts the various salvific universalisms that swarm world Adventism today. Europeans do not exclude or minimize them. On the contrary, Europe wants to dialogue with them. World Adventism are rather those who distrust and exclude "de facto" European Adventism for its atypicality. They do not want to dialogue with it except when it bends and follows them. European Adventism is sometimes called theologically cynical and too accommodating. What doesn't convince world Adventism, beyond the numbers, is this attitude of being too friendly with those considered to be our enemies and of being too critical of Adventism's compact and euphoric certainties. We could simply call it cultural realism and historical wisdom. This valuing of the particular, while distrusting alleged universalisms, happens at the grassroots level by ordinary members in their local churches. European culture is like this because it has learned this lesson the hard way from its own history. European Adventism has been positively influenced, and thus improved, by this European cultural trait.

Culture does not determine, but certainly influences, the theological and social configuration of all churches, including Adventism. Each church, like each theology, is culturally rooted and therefore bears specific historical names and surnames. It is legitimate to think that European Adventism is actually more European than Adventist. Likewise, Europeans could easily respond in the same way, that American Adventism is actually more American than Adventist, even when it strives to prove otherwise. Every theological reflection and configuration is always culturally mediated and a child of its own time. There is no neutral, ahistorical perception of God or reading of the Bible. The desire for the zero/neutral point of theological or cultural elaboration is not only a fiction but easily becomes an idolatry.

Culture is not simply the object of conscious choice, it is essentially an unconscious condition and therefore an assumption behind each individual's choice. It precedes us. At this level, we do not choose our culture; culture chooses us. It exists before us and welcomes us into life, not the other way around. Linguistically, we use the same categories of people from antiquity. But using words like God, family, and faith does not imply that the meanings are the same. Cultural homonymy is a current phenomenon. We say we worship the same God as Abraham, and nominally we are believers like Abraham, but our God is a substantively different from Abraham's God. Ours is a typically modern God. Our revival is a typical modern revival of Abraham. If Abraham were to be resurrected, he would be confused, perhaps frightened, by our individualistic, rational, functional, and contractual faith. Abraham would certainly be more comfortable with the pagans of his time because he would see them, despite major theological differences, as culturally closer to him.

Giacomo Marramao, philosopher at the University of Rome, has been a guest several times in our Villa Aurora School of Religion. He reminds us that the appeal of this cultural universalism (that he calls "identitarian universalism") is not only present in Christianity and its churches but also in the history of the West itself.[6] The paradox is that the Adventist church, while opposing modern culture, from the very beginning of its history, has been unable to offer a structural alternative. It has only proposed a thematic alternative. In fact, it has simply re-proposed the same inflexible universalism in an eschatological and ethical form, supposedly based on the Bible.

Therefore, Marramao suggests we must learn to construct what he calls a "universalism of difference," which is characterized by two essential traits.[7] First, that this new universalism must be dynamic, not static. It cannot be substantiated because religions, as well as cultures, are always on the move. Their natural allegiance to the past cannot force them to copy but only to reconfigure their past according to new challenges. Second is precisely this attention to the particular. The "universalism of differences" does not renounce to the universal but moves toward it, starting by respecting and listening to the specificity of the particular in its various forms.

---

6. Marramao, *Passage West*, 21.
7. Marramao, *Passage West*, 33.

The Trap of Theological Universalism

Marramao also reminds us that management of the particular today has become even more complex, as it is not used to dialogue with the universal but simply to oppose and protest against it. As much as universalism has been deformed by its standardization, so also the particular tends to be deformed by its alleged absolute incommensurability and substantiation. The absoluteness and intransigence of the universal is opposed to the absoluteness and intransigence of the particular. Global and local societies don't cooperate in a healthy tension but tend to exclude each other. We need to remember that the world has become heterogeneous and culturally polycentric. Thus, both the defense of a necessary and healthy universality and also the wise and flexible management of the particular have become problematic. We don't need to dismiss them but rather learn to maintain them in a profitable tension.

There is a dual tendency today. First, a radical formal universalism coexists and even facilitates strong identity-based reactionary drives. Second, the utmost defense of closed and self-referential particularisms paradoxically presuppose and reinforce the formal universalism they fight against. Indeed, globalization is an example of the former, and the hardening of religious and cultural identity of minorities is an example of the latter. And Adventism, being unaware, inscribes itself in this identity, religious hardening that tries to correct the opposite strong trend of our time, that of the formalization and standardization of culture, economics, and society.

At this point, the description of contemporary Adventism becomes complicated because of the church's persistent obsession with abstract doctrinal universalism. But it paradoxically coexists with another obsession: a closed, identity-based, tribal, religious particularism. Adventism has not one but two problems: an inflexible universalism on the theological and eschatological level, and an equally inflexible ecclesiological and missionary particularism. Neither mission nor eschatology are negative in themselves, but they are not now helping Adventism to put in dialogue our universalist aspiration and its necessary respect for particularisms. Our religious universalism (theological and administrative) is not interested in the particular, and our religious particularism is only interested in its own particular. The result is a theological and religious paradigm that tends to be schizophrenic, torn between two allegiances—universal and particular—that it cannot keep together except in a caricatured form.

European Adventism can be a resource to be valued, not an anomaly to be corrected. The inflexible theological universalism and closed, militant particularism of mainline Adventism is contrasted by European Adventism, which exhibits a "flexible theological universalism" and a "dialogical particularism." The conquering, militant, missionary Adventism, present throughout the world, is polite but unkind because it does not accept others as they are. Also, it is impaired by this inflexible universalism and its parallel, closed and distrustful particularism. European Adventism, on the other hand (and against all appearances), cultivates a kind and soft theology and eschatology, which are not dismissive of passion and conviction but have learned to be dialogical. Dialogue gives credit to the universal and the particular components of a healthy religious experience.

PART II

Vulnerability and Flourishing

9

A Reasonable Adventism

FROM ITS VERY BEGINNING, religion has been both a problem and a resource for modern Europe. Modern Europe was actually born in the seventeenth century as a radical critique of traditional religion. Europeans did not abandon religion completely though. They rather elaborated on an innovative interpretation of it, adapted to their own historical context. Even to the present, secularized Europe maintains what we could see as an oxymoron, i.e., secularized types of religion, to the point that we could say almost all forms of European religions, which were opposed ideologically to secularization or at least tried to limit it, are in fact religious forms of it. Adapting religion to its immediate sociocultural context is not necessarily a perversion. It expresses a kind of historical wisdom. Adaptation goes beyond cultural rigidity and cultural syncretism by trying to pay attention to the surrounding context without surrendering completely to it. For this reason, contemporary religions are de facto secularized religions that have metabolized and incorporated secularization as part of themselves—religions that define their profile not only in relation to their own theological premises but in relation to the external cultural context.

A "reasonable Adventism" is typical of the secularized religion in which European Adventism tries to define itself, not only in coherent relation to its own founding principles but also in relation and correspondence to the secularized society outside of it, in which its own members already live most of their lives. Even mainline Adventism, which is indeed critical of this "reasonable Adventism," is, notwithstanding, also a form of secularized religion that is unaware of this historical condition.

Starting with J. Habermas's category of post-secular,[1] let's try to briefly describe two basic principles concerning the relation between society and religion. First, religion didn't disappear with the arrival of secularization. Religions resisted secularization paradoxically in the name of secularization itself adopting typical forms of secularized religiosity. Today's forms of religiosity would appear to pre-moderns as not religions at all because of this atypical secular component integrated in the heart of today's religions. For example, one of these pivotal elements, very present in today's religions, is individualism.

Second, the return of religion in what Habermas calls "post-secular societies" doesn't entail the disappearance of secularization but rather its transformation into less radical forms. But for this reason, it becomes more transversal, diffuse, and unconscious. The same conclusion is paradoxically found in an author like Charles Taylor, who, in opposition to Habermas, has always had a critical position on secularization.[2] For Taylor, the push of secularization is inevitable. It is not over but is present in our current societies in what he calls the power of the "immanent frame." All religions are articulated within this immanent paradigm, which is the sweet and kind face of secularization spread all over in our institutions, groups, and events.

A similar ambivalence is present in the European Adventism, which is critical of the mainline, radical, and apocalyptic versions of Adventism practiced elsewhere in the world. At the same time, European Adventism defends its own interpretation of Adventism that configures itself as, what we could call, a "reasonable Adventism."

"Reasonable Adventism" sounds like a downward compromise, a sort of pruned, thinned, and purged Adventism. Actually, the opposite is true because a hypertrophic body is not necessarily more performant, as much as "bigger" is not necessarily a synonym of health or flourishing. Spanish philosopher Josep Maria Esquirol, in his beautiful book *Humà, més humà* (*Human, More Human*) reminds us that in order for somebody or something to flourish, it is necessary to recover incompleteness and vulnerability as necessary and primordial human conditions.[3] Full and plethoric entities are inappropriate and not ready to flourish because they are not touched by

---

1. Habermas, *Religion and Rationality*.
2. Taylor, *Secular Age*, 539–93.
3. Esquirol, *Humà, més humà*.

lack or a beneficial emptiness that is essential for surviving and for entering in relation. As much as persuasive and touching melodies presuppose and include silence and pauses, so healthy beings are not plethoric but intermittent and interrupted entities. They are "reasonable beings" who have learned to perceive life's systole and diastole as mechanism that support life in its contractions and expansions, in its affirmation and flexibility, in its giving and receiving in the context of the multiple relationships life offers and demands of us.

A full life is, paradoxically, an endangered life. This is why the rush to be complete is one of the worst aspirations because it not only makes us self-sufficient and happy with ourselves but it also kills in us the desire for others. Bulimia and obesity are not only eating disorders. They also have parallel cultural and sociological forms that go undiagnosed today and are precursors and facilitators of the parallel psychological dysfunctionalities. Today's societies are culturally obese. They are "aporophobic societies" that want to be full and self-sufficient and don't want to depend on anybody.

Aporophobia is a neologism created by the Spanish philosopher of the University of Valencia, Adela Cortina, to describe the "rejection of the poor."[4] It describes an adverse attitude by nonpoor against the poor, going from antipathy, contempt, disgust, and disregard to fear and hate. But behind this stigmatization of the poor hides the fear of "not having enough." The fear of being like those who "don't have enough" triggers the rush to cultural and economic obesity enhanced by the parallel bulimic mechanism of an uncontrolled and deformed desire to eat, to incorporate continually food and things that are outside and put them in our minds and bodies in order to feel secure.

Adventism, paradoxically, is not an alternative to this bulimic cultural trend. It simply expands and refines it with typical Adventist motifs and categories. We could say that mainline Adventism tends to be too plethoric and theologically aporophobic. It abhors incompleteness and vulnerability. For this same reason, obese Adventism needs to be thinned out to recover its lost erotic dimension and revive a healthy sense of incompleteness that can teach us to trust and to desire others as the incarnation of Jesus himself (see Matt 25).

So, "reasonable Adventism" means simply that. Losing some weight and discovering the value of incompleteness and vulnerability. Plethoric bodies are less resistant. Vulnerable bodies are more resistant and resilient.

4. Cortina, *Aporofobia*.

Making Adventism a "reasonable Adventist" is a kenotic process. Not muscular, heroic, and bold affirmations but vulnerable, sober, and emphatic witnessing can put Adventism back on track.

But let's come back to the initial European ambivalence concerning religion. This typical European ambivalence finds expression in one of modernity's founders, Thomas Hobbes. He was the architect of the modern state who, for reasons related to that historical context, sought to remove religion from the public sphere (Peace of Westphalia, 1648) in order to preserve peace, which was, for him, the main condition to exercise public power. This new atypical place given to religion necessarily triggered a process of secularization and a critique of traditional religion that would continue to the present and give rise to what Charles Taylor calls the "Immanent Frame."[5] This is the articulation of a religiosity from below, with the implicit presupposition of "*etsi deus non daretur*," living one's faith "as if God were not there." Along with this critical attitude, Hobbes developed a new vision of Christianity—a vision aligned with his new political project. Indeed, Hobbes is a diligent interpreter of the Bible. In both *Leviathan*,[6] his main work, and *De cive*,[7] which preceded it by only a few years, one finds veritable exegetical–theological treatises. In these texts, Hobbes achieves a true exegesis of the central texts of the Old and New Testaments. He embeds his examination with penetrating reflections in a theological project that produces a clearly delineated and coherent analysis.

From its earliest formulation, and for a few more centuries, Hobbes's reading and interpretation of the Bible would be both original and great. From an ancient text, he succeeds in elaborating a blueprint for a new, unprecedented time. Like any good interpretation, his does not link its time to ancient patterns but allows the present moment to receive its thrust and legitimacy. Thus, an ancient text can serve as a propeller toward something new. This innovative prospective in reading the Bible is immediately visible in the two books just mentioned.

On one hand, Hobbes gives birth to a new Christianity based on a creative reading of the Bible (Old and New Testaments). On the other hand, this new Christianity is entirely aligned with the modern state. In fact, his analysis serves as the logic of a modern state and reinforces its legitimacy.

---

5. Taylor, *Secular Age*, 539–93.
6. Hobbes, *Leviatano*.
7. Hobbes, *De cive*.

The Bible, as read by Hobbes with the Christianity derived from it,[8] is a strange mixture of freedom and captivity.

Hobbes's biblical hermeneutics breaks with the deterministic logic of a medieval, church-centered and group-centered approach, derived from Aristotle' social and political anthropology (*zoon politikon*) and from Christianity's relational and communitarian anthropology (community of believers). It creates an interpretation focused and based on the individual, which allows the formation of the modern state understood as the contract of individuals. A "Hobbesean state" had new characteristics and mechanisms, but it ended up chaining them both to a social contract that must be in service of the state. Unfortunately, this biblical interpretation panders to his *Leviathan* and thus absolutely and exclusively legitimates the monopoly of political force.

The modern Christianity proposed by Hobbes is more modern than Christian. This is not a problem in itself. Rather, the explanation given becomes one. Inevitably, every version of Christianity found in history interprets the Bible in accordance with its own lived context. The problem arises when one wants to represent a specific interpretation as totally biblical. They are though, circumstantial and, above all, transitory because they are tied to a particular historical period. Yet the desire is for the specific context to be definitive.

Over time, Europe refined its critique and assimilation of Christianity. Europe experienced excessive secularization in recent decades, which implies a major deconstruction of the assumptions that underpin society and culture. Thus, contemporary Europe must try to re-introduce a "reasonable version of religiosity" that can guarantee its cultural project as well as its social cohesion. One of the authors who tries to defend this urgent need for a "reasonable religion" is Jürgen Habermas. Starting from Ernst-Wolfgang Böckenförde's theorem,[9] "The secularized liberal state lives on assumptions it cannot guarantee," Habermas reintroduces as a necessary element for the survival of Europe a certain kind of religion that he calls "reasonable religion." The state, like culture and society, cannot survive solely on the basis of organization, policy assumptions, or purely economic and social management criteria. Religious and ethical relativism can end up destroying not only religiosity but also social and political institutions. For this reason,

---

8. Hobbes, *Leviatano*, see especially parts 3 and 4. See also Hobbes, *De cive*, especially part 3 on religion, chapters 15–18.

9. Böckenförde, *Formazione dello Stato*.

Habermas's is a cultural and political proposal very critical of relativism. "Reasonable" is not, in Habermas's perspective, synonymous of relativism but rather the affirmation of its overcoming.

With this argument, Habermas introduced a post-secular vision of European societies, which points to the value of being "reasonable" and its relevance, not only for religion but also for ethics and politics. A viable modern ethics is not one of all-out relativism, as is prevalent today, but neither is it built on absolute truth and values that would seek to replace it. Habermas's "third way" doesn't defend absolute rationality but the reasonableness of "ought-to-be." His "third way" also applies to politics, which he asserts will take the form of a "deliberative politics." This will arise not from secular absolutes but from reasonable dialogue among various political options. In the same way, the social structure must be built on the "reasonable," not on rigid and intransigent social ideals that often exclude and don't allow the necessary convergence of heterogeneous components of society.

In this context, an extraordinary dialogue took place between Jürgen Habermas and Cardinal Joseph Ratzinger,[10] two of the most significant intellectual figures of that time, both in Germany and internationally. It was a major event in itself, as the meeting and discussion was between two singularly influential personalities in the intellectual world of laymen and believers. But it also had even greater significance when one carefully analyzes the two talks. Amid the secularist temptation to brand all forms of religious culture as irrational regression and the fundamentalist desire to authoritatively impose the truths of a single religious faith, Habermas and Ratzinger opened up the prospect of a post-secular society[11] in which secularists and believers build up a dialogue as a method for self-discovery and not merely an instrument of a necessary compromise.

Thus Habermas's "third way" builds on the category of "reasonable" to overcome both relativism and fundamentalism. As such, it not only sobers both religion and the state, but, more importantly, makes them inclusive. In both fundamentalism and relativism, the typical exclusionary absolutism is configured and survives intact, though reversed. In fact, a deliberative politics of the "reasonable" has, as its first characteristic, that of inclusiveness. In many ways, inclusiveness precedes reasonableness. In the face of societies and churches that have become structurally heterogeneous, multicultural, and pluralistic, the sin to avoid is "worshiping" the true and absolute that

---

10. Organized by the Katholische Akademie on January 19, 2004, in Munich.

11. Ratzinger, *Etica, religione e stato liberale*.

easily become exclusive and excluding. The need to recognize those lives and ideas that do not resemble our own, but have the same right to life and recognition, necessarily leads to the transition from "true" to "true-like," and from "rational" to "reasonable."

Truth and the rationality can easily become idols we compulsively worship in our cities and churches. The bond of human and religious respect for each other forces us to a change of register. This is both theological and human wisdom. A militant call to confirm truth risks the exclusion of others. "Truth," paradoxically, tends to divide and exclude. "Reasonableness" instead tends to include and create convergence. There is not necessarily a convergence where truth is affirmed absolutely, while there is certainly more truth where convergence is made possible. It's a paradox that such exclusion occurs through a sincere but myopic call to truth. With Jesus, truth is structurally inclusive and flexible precisely because its center is not doctrinal propositions but concrete persons. Thus mainline Adventism expresses a contradiction in terms. In order to save an eschatological propositional truth, it is willing to erase everyone out of the picture. In doing so, Adventism doesn't realize that it not only erases real truth but also itself.

In this sense, European Adventism is paradoxically the most eschatological of all Adventisms. It tries to flex its eschatology, not abandon it, to include others. Especially included in these others are its own children, who often no longer attend church. European Adventism is a "reasonable Adventism" because it is inclusive. Even though Southern Adventists criticize European Adventism for its coldness and indifference, this reasonable Adventism, present in Europe, is more inclusive because it's built on ideological moderation. Real inclusiveness should be measured ideologically, not socially. For this reason, the various militant Adventisms in the world, beyond their merits, are in fact perversely exclusionary, insensitive, and indifferent to people, as was the "great" and "efficient" prophet Jonah. If social or philanthropic inclusiveness stops when others start thinking and modeling their own particular views, we can say with certainty that we are facing a fake inclusiveness. Adventism rooted in Europe—more than elsewhere—is actually a great virtue precisely because of this "ideological reasonableness" that others see as a flaw. Therefore, against all appearances and based on the importance that ideas/doctrines have for us, the more inclusive Adventism is found in Europe.

Habermas was not the one who invented the idea of reasonable identity as a mechanism that promotes coexistence and inclusion; Europe invented Habermas. This same Europe has unwittingly evangelized European Adventism into making it "reasonable." Europe has given to Adventism at least as much as Adventism has given to Europe. In missionary interaction, both hearers and preachers change. That is what has miraculously happened with European Adventism. It is not an accident that Habermas's treatise on political theory has as its subtitle *The Inclusion of the Other*.[12] The true goal of politics, even more so of religions, is to include people, not to stigmatize and push them away. In other regions of the world, Adventism is numerically larger but qualitatively smaller because it is isolated and exclusionary. European Adventism, on the other hand, is qualitatively strong though numerically smaller because Adventist friendships are often more with those outside than those on the inside. The strength of European Adventism lies not in the church but in the culture and societies that gave birth to it and with which Adventism remains in touch.

---

12. Habermas, *Inclusion of the Other*.

10

The Need for a Slow Church

ACCORDING TO GERMAN PHILOSOPHER Peter Sloterdijk,[1] societies in late modernity and those in early modernity, beyond important differences, have in common a particular element: a new understanding of time. They both have overwhelmingly prioritized time over space. Not only has space been subjugated, transformed, and deformed by the dynamism and arrogance of modern times, but modern times defines itself without any reference to space or whatever element other than itself. Society itself is born presupposing this new linear understanding of time that has transformed, for example, the way we used to create human groupings. Communities (*gemeinschaft*) in the past presupposed a cyclical time, while today's societies (*gesellschaft*) work with a linear understanding of time. The very essence of "society" (*gesellschaft*) is time understood as a linear event. The quantitative benefits of this cultural new perspective are evident, while the qualitative anomalies of this unilateral temporality are often overlooked or minimized. Sloterdijk tries to correct this imbalance—"place" over "time"—through the category of spheres,[2] which is the title of his trilogy. His books' title *Spheres* could also be understood as "Being and Space," to balance Heidegger's parallel unconcluded main work *Being and Time*,

---

1. Sloterdijk, *Kritik der Zynischen Vernunft*.
2. Sloterdijk, *Bubbles: Spheres I*; *Globes: Spheres II*; *Foams: Spheres III*.

which has involuntarily contributed to radicalize this imbalance in favor of time to the detriment of space.

The call for a slow Adventism, similar to Sloterdijk's call, is the call to temper the excessive dependence of Adventism on time, theologically and practically, in order to recuperate a beneficial sense of space. All the main categories of Adventism are too much influenced, modeled, and conditioned by a linear understanding of time, which has become a flaw from a virtue, that is deforming Adventism's beliefs and lifestyle. Dependent on this linear understanding of time are the main parallel categories we use to describe the nature of religious experience: transformation, sanctification, decision, action, goals, perseverance, growing up, movement, increase, or progress.

We are in urgent need of slowing down Adventism. And the first positive effect of taking space seriously is slowness. Slow Adventism doesn't mean to diminish Adventism and its soul, but it rather intends to refresh and regenerate it as being critical of linear temporality, to pivot Adventism eschatology and history, and to envision a new Adventism, starting from the recovery and valorization of the category of space. The main Adventist category that can help in facilitating this reorientation is the Sabbath.[3]

We should, suggests physicist Carlo Rovelli, think again about the status we have given to time and space because all we think and do is conditioned by this heavy subordination of space to time.[4] If this is true for culture in general, it is still more true for Adventism, which has the Sabbath as a central category of its whole theology. The Sabbath, generally understood by Adventism almost exclusively as a temporal category, is, in fact, a strong spatial[5] category, not only because its explicit critique of temporal linearity but particularly because it's strongly related to creation and nature. Creation and nature are space-related categories. Slowing down doesn't mean to be less but to aspire to be more; as going faster doesn't necessarily mean to reach more but could simply express a sort of temporal dependance, which is typical, according to Hartmut Rosa,[6] of today's more diffuse and transversal alienation: acceleration.

But this priority given to linear temporality, manifested in the way we create human groups (societies) or in the way we understand the Sabbath, heavily impregnates another pivotal category of today's culture: action.

---

3. Gutierrez Salazar, "Spatial Theology (Part 1)"; "Spatial Theology (Part 2)."
4. Rovelli, *Che cos'è il tempo?*, 8–21.
5. Gutierrez Salazar, "Spatial Theology (Part 3)"; "Spatial Theology (Part 4)."
6. Rosa, *Alienation and Acceleration*.

Action, understood as performative, presupposes the linearity of time. It's common to think that what we are clearly influences and directs what we do. Our actions are always the child of our being and draw their greatness or poverty from them. In fact, the opposite also happens. Over time, what we do transforms what we are. This second option has become the rule today. Action predominates over being and imposes its own rhythm and arbitrariness. Ours is an avowedly functional, pragmatic, and constructivist time. This is not necessarily a bad thing, but it becomes so when we are unaware of the side effects, and especially when we see it as a unique and universal model.

There is a clear imbalance in contemporary culture that, since the Renaissance, has prioritized action over being, function over stability. As Aaron Y. Gourevitch says, modernity starts when time/history is chosen as its pivotal category.[7] This modern understanding of time is widely present—from art to technology, from ethics to theology—and has become an addiction. It has turned virtue into compulsion. We cannot help but do something. Our being is measured by the achievements of actions, programs, and goals that we give ourselves to prove our worth. From the lack of being, the poverty of knowing how to be, we try to compensate with even more compulsive activity.

Action, whether religious or secular, has become a real addiction. It starts automatically, without delay and without being able to think about its assumptions, its configuration, its relationships, and the unforeseen effects it generates.

Above all, compulsion to action is considered a great virtue. Getting busy and doing is regarded as nobility of spirit, involvement, and responsibility. Its problematic nature is not perceived; it's even offered as a model to follow. We all suppose and affirm within ourselves that doing is always a virtue. Laziness and not doing anything is instead the "mother (source) of all evils." This is what Byung-Chul Han describes as an "Achievement Society."[8] In an achievement society, doing, and doing more and more, is not only ethically virtuous but also anthropologically appropriate. That keeps us busy, producing results that justify not only what we do, but also who we are. This produces the mechanicalness (sold as regularity) and compulsion (smuggled in as responsibility) of contemporary human actions.

Unfortunately, Adventism is no exception to this. In fact, it is a clear example of this cultural performance model. Adventist doctrinal alternatives

7. Gourevitch, "Postface," 257–76.
8. Han, *Burnout Society*, 8–11.

(Sabbath, eschatology, lifestyle, etc.) are really only formal alternatives in that they merely express and promote a functional, pragmatic, and militant faith. Mainline Adventism has made this "performance" model its most important reference point. Adventism has been, since its inception, pragmatic and concrete, but it is more radical today. This fact doesn't depend on what Adventism believes or says—it believes and says the same things it used to believe and to say—but it depends on the new radical pragmatic social context that Adventism unconsciously breaths and assimilates, and which it is unable to resist because it ignores and minimizes it.

Our leaders believe that Adventist faith preserves and reinforces its identity with this performative model, to which Adventism uncritically and unconsciously bends. But actually, the opposite happens. It's not Adventism that flourishes but only the Adventist model of performance. This means that only the cultural model of performance is reinforced. European Adventism is a happy exception to this. Despite itself, and sometimes with little conviction, it tries to personify quality over quantity, substance over form, dialogue over isolation.

Sociologists Federico Chicchi of the University of Bologna and Anna Simone of the University of Rome gave a presentation of their book *The Achievement Society*[9] in our School of Religion at Villa Aurora in Florence. They reminded us that we are facing a new phenomenon. It is not the classic disciplined, conscious, and responsible activism of our parents, our pioneers, or even prototypical puritans. This obsession with doing has produced three anthropologically important changes.

- *First*, norms have been internalized. Whereas in the past, the call to do came from outside, today it comes from within ourselves because we are the ones who are the implacable judges of ourselves and the actions we have to perform. We have moved, Foucault reminds us, from a "disciplinary society" to a "performance society," in which individuals become their own artisans.

- *Second*, society has ceased to be that in-between space that offers individuals the opportunity to propose and experience alternative paths to the model. Society has stopped being normative from a religious point of view but has become heavily normative from the perspective of the anthropological model and the actions it urges. Society

---

9. Chicchi, *Società della prestazione*.

demands more and more without providing the tools to succeed, imposing higher and higher standards with our own consent.

- *Third*, this urgency to do, which comes from individuals themselves and from society with its performance models, wears out the best in us. It forces us to produce only a greater quantity of results that, however, hide an increasingly compromised and reduced human quality. A vicious circle is thus configured. The less we are (ontologically and anthropologically), the more we are tempted to do more things, intending to compensate for this anthropological deficit. But the more we act compulsively, the more our being is impoverished.

This pattern of performance has another devastating effect on believers: it erases passion and imagination. The performance model produces a major anthropological transformation. Individuals become bureaucrats, like machines, and ethically reliable individuals because they are predictable as they show no passion or imagination. This is what Byung-Chul Han describes as a "society without eros."[10] Performance societies are precise, efficient, and disciplined, but they lack "eroticism." They are human spaces where "eros agonizes."[11] If we apply this description to mainline Adventism, we see that Adventist militants often appear as predictable bureaucrats, doing only what the programs demand. We have in front of us only soldiers without *eros*, flattened only to the duties they are called upon to fulfill regularly and without questioning.

But there is a more important loss in the disappearance of *eros*: the loss of others. *Eros* comes not from ourselves but from the presence and desires of others. One's own desire (Lacan) is to be desired by others. All this has disappeared from mainline Adventism. Our euphoria is self-generated, not derived from the presence of others. Only the other, the desire for the other, maintains the eroticism and love of life. Attention to others slows down life and action, thus breaking the linearity of performance patterns. A performance action does not have excessive speed as its main defect. This is a secondary aspect. The main defect is the loss of the other, of listening to and speaking with others.

Adventism has never really been attentive to others, except when they become Adventist. But in a time of extreme missionary militancy like ours, the other has disappeared even more. The rejection of dialogue, or

---

10. Han, *Eros in agonia*, 20–21.
11. Han, *Eros in agonia*, 31–32.

ecumenism, is the sublimation of our inability to recognize the other. The dilemma remains if we Adventists are anti-ecumenical as a refined sublimation of our genetic incapacity to consider others or, because we are anti-ecumenical, our capacity to be with others has been radically atrophied.

We have become like the prophet Jonah: great missionaries but not loving others. In fact, we see in others only a danger. We have become a narcissistic church, thinking of ourselves as all-sufficient. The other slows us down, disorganizes our plans, introduces unpredictability—all elements that a compulsive mission cannot afford to include or even consider. We love our plans more than others, as did Jonah the prophet.

Our obsession with doing has not only made us lose others, it also makes us lose reality. We are a church living in a parallel reality, a non-reality. Compulsive militancy thinks that reality is negligible and that what matters is its own project. Our own project is the true reality. There is a disarming naiveté and candor in compulsive militancy. Compulsive militants choose, without hesitation, their own mission, thus forgetting that it is reality—life, people, and history—that validates or invalidates the claims of their own religious project.

Psychoanalyst Arnold Goldberg points out that "secondary" defense mechanisms, typical of neurosis, sacrifices ego integrity but keeps contact with reality intact.[12] "Primary" defense mechanisms, on the other hand, sacrificed the connection with reality to keep the ego intact. The intact ego, disconnected from reality, is not intact, however. In fact, psychosis represents this: the break with the sense of reality. Goldberg analyzes an anthropological and psychiatric transformation that starts at the point of this new performance subject. To be performative, at some point "repression" (secondary defense mechanism) is replaced by "splitting" (primary defense mechanism). That splitting implies and involves a detachment from reality. How, then, could one be performative and detached from reality at the same time? This would be the "new perversions," psychological configurations that make a legitimate thing (work, commitment, responsibility, etc.) a way to detach oneself from reality by creating parallel realities aligned with one's obsessions. So, we will be faced with psychological and anthropological disorders that were once dysfunctional but today are not necessarily so. This maintained functionality is not a sign of health but rather a sign of a psychic "split" that sooner or later explodes.

---

12. Goldberg, *Problem of Perversion*, 23–26.

We could say that the pragmatic-neurotic Adventist of the past who remained attached to reality has been replaced by the performative-split Adventist, who has lost touch with reality and, through a dissociative mechanism, lives in a parallel reality with, unfortunately, an increased functionality that doesn't allow one to perceive this deep anomaly.

European Adventism identifies less or not at all with this compulsive militancy. But what appears as a flaw to others is partly a virtue—the virtue of thinking of faith in a new way. That is what we could call a "slow Adventism," which resists the obsession with numbers and results. Slow does not just mean less compulsive. Being at the grassroots means an Adventism that values others. Slow is not an ethical virtue but an anthropological attitude that comes from including others—others from our own communities but also from groups other than our own. The more we include others and allow ourselves to be challenged by their lives and questions, the slower our journey of life and faith becomes. The faster and more high-performing we are, the more certain it is that we have lost sight of others. Lamberto Maffei, an Italian neurologist, in his book *Praise of Slowness*, reminds us that a slower time is necessary not only from a social and cultural perspective but also for bodily and neurological needs.[13]

"Slow church," as embodied in European Adventism, is an asset, not a problem. The mainline Adventist church, with its high performativity model, hides a great fragility. A slow church learns, counterintuitively, to perhaps baptize less and "waste" more time in relationships, not only among members within the community but also with people and friends from other communities who represent the human richness and anthropological stratum capable of tempering our eschatological and apocalyptic obsessions and compulsions.

---

13. Maffei, *Elogio della lentezza*, 45–73.

11

Centripetal and Centrifugal Adventism

THE CHURCH IS A community of believers who, through faith in Christ, find in the association of believers space and stimulus for their spiritual and human growth and flourishing. This definition of the church envisions two overlapping but distinct entities, at times in tension: the church as a body and the individual believers. There is no church without individual believers, just as there is no association of believers that does not create some form of church over time.

While initially, a church is known by the dynamism of its members, as time goes on, members are recognized by their adherence to the church organization's beliefs and practices. Thus, church structure tends to subordinate individual believers. The church—any church—manifests in this its bulimia of meaning and power. But this natural, historical evolution does not constitute an ironclad determinism. Wise, flexible, and mature congregations manage to maintain, along with affirming the institutional church, the flourishing of individual members. This, unfortunately, could not be the case with Adventism. The Seventh-day Adventist church demonstrates a worrisome *hyper*trophy of the church structure and a lamentable *hypo*trophy of its members.

According to Nobel Prize economists Daron Acemoglu and James A. Robinson, in their book *Why Nations Fail*, hypertrophic institutions are those that seem to be in good health because of the resources they have and administer, but this quantitative strength is only superficial in the sense that it hides instead the incapacity of creating richness.[1] In fact, hypertrophic institutions are lazy bodies that are "extractive," say Acemoglu and Robinson. Not being able to create richness by themselves, they expropriate and usurp richness created by individuals whom they should instead recognize, respect, and motivate. In other words, "extractive institutions" are "centripetal entities," which are like parasites living off others' lives. They are not creative but maintainers, not visionaries but customary, not trusting but controlling, not biophilic but necrophiliac social, economic, or religions entities. Why do they manage to survive? Because their expropriating character is dissimulated and covered by an institutional and philanthropic paternalism. Centripetal institutions make us believe that they are essential, crucial, and indispensable in guaranteeing individuals' well-being. They pretend to take care of people when, in fact, they are living thanks to what they get from them.

"Inclusive institutions," according to Acemoglu and Robinson, are characterized instead by two particular traits: first, for their commitment in favor of the creative forces within the system; second, for the capacity of remaining thin and functional mediators in that process, not the final recipients of the benefits created by individuals.[2] "Inclusive institutions" are, for this reason, "centrifugal institutions" characterized by flexibility and adaptability in benefit of the creative forces of the system.

For historical, institutional (and unfortunately), theological reasons, the Adventist church sets itself up as a church against its members. It certainly does not do so in a crude, disjointed way but in a refined way, through initiatives and proposals that it considers useful to the members but are, in fact, only partially useful at best. Adventist church hierarchy tends to consider its members only insofar as they are useful for the church's ends. This is exemplified in Adventism's lack of meaningful ecumenical dialogue and interface with the outside world.

Lack of healthy ecumenical dialogue contributes to the stunted growth of its members, fomenting religious and cultural impoverishment. This opposition to ecumenism comes not only from the top of the institution but, unfortunately, has been internalized by members themselves, allured by shiny-but-ill-advised militancy.

If dialogue with other groups and denominations is absent, individual members do not have the opportunity to compare themselves with others

---

1. Acemoglu, *Why Nations Fail*, 34–53.
2. Acemoglu, *Why Nations Fail*, 34–53.

and verify that what they receive from their own church nourishes them or doesn't. In its anti-ecumenical attitude, the church privileges itself, not the individuals, precisely because it aims to rigidly defend group identity, not the welfare of individuals.

Unfortunately, mainline Adventism, with its widespread, across-the-board anti-ecumenism, ultimately burdens and stiffens the church and simultaneously infantilizes the religious and intellectual agency of individual believers.

European Adventism differs significantly from this model. It begins instead from assumptions that recognize the spiritual gifts of other faith communities (including the Catholic community) and affirms individual believers as active agents in their faith experiences. There are two manifestations of this: first, at the hermeneutical level, and second, at the ecclesiological level. Elaborating a critique of what we might call "hermeneutical positivism" and its parallel "ecclesiological positivism," which predominate in mainline Adventism, European Adventism builds on an inclusive reading of the Bible and an inclusive understanding of the church. All this is based on the conviction that Adventism, at most, interprets only part of the Bible and that the Adventist church, at best, is *part* of God's kingdom, not the *whole* kingdom.

"Biblical positivism," which includes but is not limited to biblical fundamentalism (inerrancy), starts from a reductive concept of the Bible through, for example, the all-out defense of the principle of *sola scriptura*. The Bible is self-explanatory—essentially understandable and transparent in itself. Most importantly, it requires no substantive connection or interaction with the outside world, society, or culture to fully articulate its message. It connects to society and culture to establish its historical–temporal framing. This way of reading the Bible is anomalous for two reasons:

First, it presents the Bible as a compact, homogeneous unity, emphasizing continuity over discontinuity, complementarity over tension, and synthesis over fragmentation. It presumes that God and truth are unitary realities. If so, the Bible must also bear those characteristics. The most common phrases to affirm this first conviction are "the Bible never contradicts itself," "any contrasts are only apparent," or "apparent contrasts belong to the human part of the Bible." But the most distinctive feature of this first belief is the thought that the Bible is structurally clear, never opaque. Its meaning is perfectly transparent and self-evident. These are readers, who by the brokenness they bring with them, introduce a lack of clarity that must be refuted.

Second, this way of reading imagines the Bible as an autonomous reality. It envisions the Bible's interaction with the world outside itself as introducing discontinuity, not continuity; tension, not complementarity; and rupture rather than integration. This approach asserts that the Bible is not dependent on any human realities. The mantra of this conviction is "*sola scriptura*—the Bible and the Bible alone." This reading of Scripture understands the principle of *sola scriptura* in its most exclusivist and self-referential connotation.

Biblical positivism, starting from the assumption of the Bible's purity, lives by the conviction that we must protect Scripture, preserving it from all manipulation and distortion. The longer the Bible remains in contact with realities foreign to it, the greater the risk of contamination. The Bible must be protected and safeguarded in its compactness because this fact guarantees its truth and its divine inspiration. In this view, the Bible appears monolithic and homogeneous because it has been detached from everything else—even from life itself. But, vice versa, the Bible is detached from everything else precisely because it has become monolithic, compact, and inflexible. The more monolithic an entity is, the more abstract it becomes—and the more abstract, the more monolithic.

To this reductive biblical positivism (a hermeneutic typical of mainline Adventism that European Adventism disputes) is added the parallel and complementary "ecclesiocentrism" that has become even more rigid and radical in recent years because it is not only theological in nature but has also become administrative. This reinforces a strong, unwavering partnership between "biblical positivism" and "ecclesiological positivism," which are both centripetal movements that deeply impoverish Adventism.

One result is that Adventism ends up attributing to itself as a church attributes that belong only to the Bible as a foundational text. The church becomes as sacred, absolute, unchallengeable, and untouchable as the Bible itself (and vice versa) because the Bible, by definition a text of all and for all, becomes only the reflection and extension of a specific community and its narrow and limited interpretation.

The European Adventist church, on the other hand, stands against this trend, instead espousing a more open hermeneutic and ecclesiology. Faith is not only *affirmation* but also requires a good deal of *reflection*. The necessary practice of faith, without reflection, easily becomes activism and missionary compulsion. Mission must not be an escape, even less the sublimation of an inadequate, militant faith that is afraid to think.

Unilateral and short-sighted centripetal movements and strategies of a church or of other institutions should be continuously assessed and checked. As time goes by, innovative, even revolutionary, initiatives tend to become closed and self-referential. To understand the critical importance of thinking and not just acting, consider the example of the financialization of the economy and its analogous reversal of system and people in favor of systems. French economist Thomas Piketty provides such analysis in his book *The Capital in the Twenty-First Century*.[3]

Piketty's book stems from the observation and need to defend a commonsense idea hidden by the rise of financial capitalism: high income and substantial capital in the hands of a minority, coupled with slowing growth, does not serve the establishment of a democratic society and the welfare of most of its citizens. This fact is obvious. Less obvious is how we got here. We got here precisely by skipping reflection and analysis that should continually monitor and assess the economic and social processes of our time.

We live, Piketty argues, in a society that watches impassively, and in many cases willingly, as capital flows to a small elite who determine society's fate. Until the 1700s, humanity inhabited a world in which change was very rare. The conditions of people's lives, in the long run, were almost always determined by their starting point; no individual merit could break the bonds of birth. From the beginning of the 1800s, however, industrialized society seems to get moving. Here, people begin to truly become the center of their possible futures. Before the outbreak of the Great War, everything undergoes an acceleration that maintains its momentum until the 1970s. Then comes Thatcher and Reagan, and the hands of the clock seem to leap backward. From the late 1800s until the gilded 1970s, work was more than the legacy that could guarantee high standards of living. Almost without realizing it, the nearly century-long trend of labor (therefore, laborers) earning more than capital/income (systems) has now been reversed. Capital is growing at the expense of labor, which has become and is becoming more and more precarious and poorly paid.

Moving to the religious level, we can certainly say that, for more than a century, Adventism served individual believers. People grew up and found in Adventism the proper environment to develop their faith and make their lives flourish—the church in service of its members. Today, this trend

3. Piketty, *Capital*.

seems to have reversed. Adventist church structure grows and believers decline—members in service of the church.

What Piketty says about financial capitalism and its strong push to leave people behind for the benefit of capital and large rents and assets can be applied to institutional Adventism today, which thinks more about keeping itself alive than about promoting the flourishing of its members. In this sense, European Adventism represents a levee to this pervasive trend in that it tries to build and promote not a muscular, identity-driven church but a "kenotic," open, incomplete, sober, and flexible "church" that serves and makes room for the questions and aspirations of individual believers.

12

A Post-Whitean Adventism

Today's Seventh-day Adventist Church is being held back by the same prophetic figure who initially gave it its dynamism. This, I contend, is primarily because of linguistic and conceptual misunderstandings. The modern Adventist Church uses Ellen G. White not to adapt to new contexts and realities but to prevent the church from adapting, instead aligning it with a tradition that has remained, in significant ways, fixed in time.

It's paradoxical that an author, whose thought is centered on the categories of conflict and dynamism, is misused to cancel both, defending at the end the rigidity of Adventism as a closed and a purist system. A true and consistent understanding of conflict, argues Chantal Mouffe, creates a different understanding of politics that she calls "agonistic pluralism,"[1] in which the central task of democracy is that of permitting conflicts. Opponents are neither companions nor enemies but adversaries among whom exists a conflictual consensus. This is the basis of what Mouffe calls "agonistic politics,"[2] the only possible politics today in a fragmented sociocultural scenario, characterized by three important traits: first, the presupposition of an impossible synthesis of all the components of a system; second, the undeniable incompleteness of each component in the system; and third, the irreversible plurality within a system. Conflict becomes, then, not only

---

1. Mouffe, *Democratic Paradox*, 8–17.
2. Mouffe, *Agonistics*, 1–18.

a central political category but a cultural category that allows us to maintain systems, secular or religious, as open systems. This is why, writes French psychoanalyst Miguel Benasayag in his book *The Praise of Conflict*, persons and communities are impaired not by conflicts but rather for the removal of conflicts typical of human life.[3]

Max Weber identified two guiding figures—traceable social patterns or archetypes—present in the emergence and establishment of modern human groups, including churches.[4] In the first one, the "prophet" is characterized by charisma, creativity, and vision. Prophetic figures are foundational and provide forward momentum. Prophets create new paths and provide new perspectives. Second, the "priest" serves a preservationist role. Priests are called to manage and protect that which has been hard-won over time. This figure's task is not to increase but to guard what one has. Both figures, in different ways and at different times, are important and essential in the identity-building process of any group.

The problem with E. G. White is that she is called a prophet but serves in Adventism rather as a priest—a figure who functionally maintains and protects an identity that must be kept pure. In the priestly role ascribed to her by the Adventist church, White no longer pushes forward but backward, no longer creates but hinders, no longer allows experimentation but stigmatizes it. She is no longer a vanguard figure but a rearguard figure. This does not derive from White herself but from an institution and a community that uses her as a pretext for staying put.

European Adventism, for various reasons, has articulated a different relationship with White—certainly a more critical and selective relationship. To some extent, the European Adventist church reads her less and knows little about her, but nevertheless has developed with her a more realistic and wise relationship. It contends reasonably that a community should not impose its prophet on the world outside but also shouldn't do it within Adventism. It has persuasive arguments to do so in the context of the new social and cultural circumstances we live in now. That is especially true when the prophet does not facilitate but burdens its community's relationship with the outside world. Let's mention some key ways European Adventism implicitly uses when it reads and explains E. G. White and her work.

The first implicit assumption is that at a functional level, a prophet is not above the possibility of making mistakes. A prophet can err. Adventism

---

3. Benasayag, *Elogio del conflitto*, 73–87.
4. Weber, *Sociology of Religion*, 46–59

abandoned biblical inerrancy with difficulty, and it would be tragically paradoxical to ascribe to E. G. White prophetic inerrancy. Unfortunately, that happened in the past. For example, A. T. Jones, one of the main figures at the General Conference session in Minneapolis 1888, used to explicitly attribute to White "verbal inspiration" and "inerrancy."[5] The Bible itself rejects the idea; more than a few times, true prophets erred and were called to task.

Second, at a structural level, the prophetic role is bound by a kind of unilateralism: a prophet could be functionally correct and make no mistake, but still, his profile has built-in limitations. No prophet has a complete view of faith or history. Every prophet, however acclaimed, has blind spots. Biblical prophetism compensates for this by introducing a plurality of prophetic voices, temperaments, sensibilities, and theological projects that Adventism simply does not have. More than the prophet as an individual, it is the global phenomenon—prophethood—that can and should constitute prophetic truth or falsehood, relevance or irrelevance. If all biblical prophecy were embodied by, interpreted by, and limited to Elijah, for instance, we would have mediocre prophethood—not because of Elijah himself but because of the lack of other alternative prophetic figures. While the biblical prophetic witness is great and noble because of the plurality it expresses, Adventist prophethood focused on White is a poorer prophetic witness because it is based in a unique person. It has the added problem of no longer being relevant in many areas and fronts because of temporal distance.

Third, at a level of temporal relevance, a prophet is current at a specific time. The role of a prophet is inseparable from a present truth, which reflects a historical context—a definite time and place. Ellen G. White is no longer a current prophet. The widespread use of her writings to settle ethical or religious questions is like using a nineteenth-century biology text to describe life processes in nature rather than considering modern scientific advances and understandings. White is a prophet of the nineteenth century. The themes, arguments, and the tenor of her writing belong to another time; they no longer correspond to our own.

Prophets have always had a two-part applicability. The first level is the historical immediacy of a prophet's addressing events closely related to their current context. The words of the prophet Jeremiah, spoken at the end of the seventh century BCE, were no more applicable to the sixth century BCE because his call to surrender to the Babylonians, for example, would have been anachronistic and essentially wrong.

---

5. Knight, *Search for Identity*, 98–100.

A Post-Whitean Adventism

The second layer of prophetic applicability has a universal reach. This comprises directions and perspectives characteristic of prophethood that retain a timeless validity, but in a general sense, not in terms of concrete, specific choices and strategies. The universal validity of prophetic principles and directions, while necessarily more general, is no less important and binding. Adventists' problem with E. G. White is applying her first-level validity to second-level concerns. This is impossible. White is in many respects a prophet from another time. For contemporary readers, her authority can only be that of the second level—an authority of general and of universal direction, not necessarily of specific and concrete choices.

The question for the Adventist church is whether it can reimagine its approach to E. G. White. Can it recognize, thanks to her influence, the emergence of new issues, themes, motives, challenges, and social, psychological, and cultural dynamics that she did not and could not know? European Adventism offers this possibility and should be seen not as part of the problem but as part of a solution to forging a new kind of relationship with Adventism's prophet.

The project of renovating or overhauling a faith tradition is threatened not only by indifference but also by individual and corporate hardening. It is not an easy undertaking. But visionary movements have tried, including the post-Marxist, socialist political vision elaborated by Chantal Mouffe and Ernesto Laclau—their so called "radical democracy."[6] The thought of Laclau and Mouffe is generally referred to as post-Marxist. Both participated in the student movement of the 1960s and hypothesized an alliance with the working class to create a new society. They reject the Marxist idea that economic determinism and class struggle are fundamental reference points for social dynamics. They instead emphasize the importance of triggering radical democratization and pluralistic antagonism in which social conflicts can be harmoniously expressed by replacing the classic class-struggle motif with contemporary issues and currents such as the environmental crisis, feminism, and minority rights—particularly LGBTQ+ rights.

Just as Mouffe and Laclau envisioned post-Marxist socialism, not by abandoning Marx but by reading him in the light of new issues, "post-Whitean" Adventism might mean not abandoning E. G. White or leaving her to the pages of history but rather reading her in the light of issues and events she never envisioned: secularization, nuclear danger, environmental crises, multiculturalism, populism, gender fluidity, globalization, autonomy and

---

6. Mouffe, *Hegemony and Social Strategy*.

self-determination of individuals, social heterogeneity, political polycentrism, relevance of a non-religious ethic, artificial intelligence, economic inequality, etc.

Ellen G. White does not have the final word on the world, history, the church, or even the Bible. She does not even define how Adventists should read the Bible today. We certainly cannot overlook—or worse, ignore—her reading of the Bible and the broad directions of her interpretation. But to identify her reading of Scripture as the reading we must have today not only makes us religiously and anthropologically lazy but elevates White to a sacrality we cannot grant. It is not enough to say that White does not contradict the Bible or that she recognizes the superiority of the Bible over her writings. If we accept her interpretations as definitive, complete, and always relevant, we are in fact placing her above Scripture. This is not only improper but ecclesiologically unproductive.

Take, for example, two parables in Matt 13 that White comments on—the parable of the "hidden treasure" and the "pearl of great price." She makes them synonymous in her interpretation, the treasure and the pearl referring to God and the value of his kingdom.

In fact, for her, the hidden treasure is the word of God in the first parable (Matt 13:44):

> The Word of God . . . is an inexhaustible Treasure.[7]

But in the second parable (Matt 13:45–46), the parable of the "pearl of great price," it is God incarnate in Christ who is, for her, the pearl to be sought:

> Christ himself is the Pearl of great price.[8]

E. G. White makes these two parables fully parallel and synonyms attributing in both cases the value only to God, Jesus, and his kingdom, not to humans. A closer reading, however, indicates that these parables are not at all synonymous. If the first parable of the treasure is theocentric, the second one, in contrast, is an anthropocentric parable in that the "kingdom of heaven" (God) is the merchant who seeks pearls he does not have. The pearl therefore cannot represent God in the second parable. It represents humanity and the intrinsic value God places upon all people.

---

7. White, *Christ's Object Lessons*, 109.
8. White, *Christ's Object Lessons*, 115.

So White cannot be for European Adventism a point of arrival, only a point of departure. Starting from her, but also from other historical, cultural, religious, and biblical vantage points, it is up to us to go further, to create a thought structure that more fully responds to the emerging challenges of our time. Even for the Bible, there are in it motives, categories, and perspectives she was unable to see and perceive because of the particular interpretative lens with which she read the Bible.

Looking from a different perspective, reading E. G. White has produced not only a more theologically homogeneous community but, unfortunately, a more wary, suspicious, and, at times, even a verbally aggressive church. Time and our prophet have made us more cynical and distrustful. End-times witnessing doesn't need to have these characteristics. It should, instead, be impregnated with what French philosopher Anne Dufourmantelle calls "the power of sweetness."[9] We don't necessarily need another prophet, but certainly a different "prophetic voice, timbre and inflection."[10]

---

9. Dufourmantelle, *Potenza della dolcezza*, 14–23.
10. Dufourmantelle, *Potenza della dolcezza*, 17.

13

A Post-Apocalyptic Adventism

MODERN ADVENTISM HAS BEEN radicalized and misshapen by its apocalyptic vision. In the denomination's early history, it provided eager anticipation for the future and the second return of Christ—one of the movement's defining characteristics. This radicalization and malformation have resulted from theological and temporal misunderstandings.

Eschatology (apocalypticism) is not in itself an absolute value. In Adventism, it's a central and primordial value, which needs, however, to be balanced and checked from within and from outside. From within, through the continuous assessment and dialogue with other theological and religious components present in Adventism. From outside, by checking the correspondence between our eschatological motives with the external reality of history and the concrete lives of people. Adventist apocalypticism is today challenged because it is not generating hope, neither for Adventists inside nor for non-Adventists outside. Eschatological conviction and coherence cannot substitute hope as the main criterion for assessing the value and health of apocalyptic pronouncements.

According to Reinhardt Koselleck, the future we are dealing with is not generating hope.[1] It has become a *"vergangene zukunft,"* a "past future," which is born old, doesn't create newness, or open new horizons. It is, according to Miguel Benasayag, an anxiety-filled and fearful future, bent on

---

1. Koselleck, *Futuro passato*.

itself, which only knows and aspires to prolong the superficial well-being of the present into tomorrow, hates temporal surprises, and necessarily creates only "sad passions" instead of hope.[2] What Koselleck and Benasayag say about today's societies applies perfectly to Adventism. And this fact shows that we better not play the "Adventist exceptionalism" card so naively and easily. Our eschatology is not, unfortunately, part of the solution but has become part of the problem. We are equal and, like our contemporaries, face despair and aspire to hope. We should avoid being Manicheans in considering non-Adventists as desperate and Adventists as hopeful. Despair and hope are mingled in the world as much as in Adventism. Our movement should learn to configure itself as a "kenotic apocalypticism," a soft, sober, kind voice, not as a boasting, fanatic, and arrogant apocalypticism. It's what Baptist theologian Miguel Angel De La Torre does when he speaks about "embracing hopelessness" as the thermometer of true eschatology.[3] British philosopher Terry Eagleton gets the idea of a kenotic eschatology from a secular perspective, when he speaks about the urgent need of having "hope without optimism."[4]

Over time, values can become obsessions, and affirmations of truth can give way to theological cynicism. In its transformation from movement to institution, Adventism failed to adequately cultivate a thorough theology of hope, either for itself or for others. Instead, longing for the future turned into obsession with the future, and waiting became a preoccupation with the end. Apocalypticism now functions in Adventism not as a source of hope for the world or a means of connecting with others over common struggles and shared problems but as an excuse to withdraw from others and to form judgments of them. It is a purist and tribalistic view of the gospel reduced to slogans by one-sided militants and identitarian Adventists who are frozen in time and have become eschatological narcissists.

Today's mainline Adventism is shot through with "eschatological illiteracy," which characterizes not only those disinterested in the end and the future but also those obsessed with the end. In the former, there is a deficit; in the latter, an excess of future-focus. "Emotional illiteracy," a parallel condition, presents as apparent, superficial, emotional indifference, which is compensated for at a different level by affective hyper-investment—an affective fixation. Emotionally illiterate people do not lack emotions. Rather,

2. Benasayag, *Epoca delle passioni tristi*.
3. De La Torre, *Embracing Hopelessness*.
4. Eagleton, *Hope Without Optimism*.

they do not exhibit them in situations that call for an emotional response but display them in the wrong places, at the wrong times, and with the wrong interlocutors. Similarly, eschatological illiterates are marked by a mixture of insensitivity, impassivity, indifference, coldness, disregard, even disdain for the future of others. Along with it comes a surprising, intense, and disproportionate passion, boundless focus, and maniacal care for their own future and the future of their tribe or church.

The prophet Jonah offers an archetypical example of this "emotional and eschatological illiteracy." He was as great a missionary as we would consider anyone who successfully converted an entire major city of antiquity, comparable to New York, Milan, Barcelona, or Manila. But he cared nothing for the people of Nineveh themselves. He displayed no concern, no positive emotion. The Ninevites' fate was ultimately insignificant to him. In contrast to his affection deficit for the thousands of inhabitants of the city, Jonah displayed an intense, boundless, and disproportionate affection for his plant, which died overnight. He held God responsible for the plant's death. Jonah loved plants more than people, not unlike many Adventists today who, radiating eschatological illiteracy, hold in higher regard their doctrines about the end than the end of the people they address.

In contrast, the European Adventist church has cultivated, beyond its own limitations and contradictions, a more sober, inclusive, and measured view of apocalypticism. This may arise, in part, from its not sharing the enthusiasm the worldwide Adventist church has shown, for example, in the distribution of the most apocalyptic Adventist book ever, *The Great Controversy*. The work is extremely divisive in its themes and language and has become even more polemical and aggressive in Adventism's use of it today.

But mainly, I think, the reason is that European Adventism believes radical Adventist apocalypticism lives by a blunder—the solecism of ignoring that between us and others are not only differences and separation but also a shared, common humanity. Apocalypticism and eschatology at their core demand universality and inclusiveness of outlook, not a focus on particularities and exclusivisms.

Unfortunately, the Adventist eschatological ethos has learned to live and feed only on conviction, consistency, and militancy without the ability to add flexibility, relationality, vulnerability, and dialogue. The resulting eschatology is true but abrasive, relevant but one-sided, convincing but unwise. Communicated without wisdom, the world does not improve—it only creates and amplifies chaos and division.

A Post-Apocalyptic Adventism

Therefore, post-apocalyptic Adventism does not have to cease being apocalyptic. It requires balancing Adventism's strong apocalyptic inclinations with other biblical themes on the one hand with new sociocultural contexts on the other. When considering biblical attestation, it is worth remembering that the Old Testament, for example, has not one but two versions of eschatology: apocalyptic and messianic. Apocalyptic literature is a distinctive combination of several fundamental axioms, including the belief in the imminent end of history correlated with the notion of "judgment." The first major explosion of apocalypticism dates back to the Hellenistic era, including early Enochian literature, for example. But the apocalyptic worldview actually predates this period. Its greatest expression is found in the book of Daniel and, even earlier, in the Prophets. All the prophets introduced apocalyptic sections into their writings through the motifs of "day of the Lord," "judgment," or "wrath of God." This is the case, for example, with Isaiah's so-called "great apocalypse" (Isa 24–27) and "little apocalypse" (Isa 34–35).

"Messianism," on the other hand, represents a second way of understanding the future, one not based on the category of "judgment" but rather on the expectation of redemption and fullness of life introduced by the Messiah. The main messianic motifs are "fullness," "completion," or "flowering." It is important to remember that the messianic worldview does not begin with Christianity, with Christ as Messiah. Messianism explodes within Christianity because Christ is the long-awaited Messiah. But the messianic worldview is already present in all the Prophets. The most messianic of all the Old Testament books is Isaiah (see Isa 11:1–9).

While hints of apocalyptic and messianic thought can be found in earlier periods, it is only with the biblical prophets that apocalypticism and messianism receive their first coherent and balanced articulation. The explosion of apocalypticism and messianism in the Hellenistic and Christian eras introduces an ambivalent situation: both eschatological visions flourish, but they tend toward one-sidedness and disconnectedness. In this regard, Old Testament eschatology remains a foundational paradigm, not only for its openness to the future but especially because of its extraordinary ability to keep these two forms—apocalypticism and messianism—together in tension. For this reason, no eschatology can be balanced if it unilaterally privileges only one of these two forms.

An example of this balance comes in Isa 2, in which both eschatological dimensions occupy the same chapter: in the first part (verses 1–5), a "messianic" description of eschatology, and in the second part (verses 6–22), an "apocalyptic" version. Both coexist side by side. The New Testament wisely maintains this balance. The messianic aspect of Christianity is perfectly embodied in the four Gospels (see Luke 4:16–21), and its apocalyptic dimension is perfectly visible (primarily, but not only) in the book of Revelation.

To its detriment, Adventism was born and matured with essentially one of the two forms of eschatology—the apocalyptic one. It has always struggled to include and remain in tension with messianism's eschatological vision. It is a fundamental weakness of Adventism—an eschatological church—that its outsized, disproportionate emphasis on apocalypticism, makes it eschatologically unbalanced.

Historical-contextual considerations serve as reminders that no church has a monopoly on the truth concerning the end times. The doctrine of the end (eschatology) is more human than divine, no less so in Adventism. The doctrine is divine only indirectly as it pertains to the Bible. But it is necessarily human in its formulation. God is sacred, his Word is sacred, not the doctrine we construct from it. Doctrines must always be rearticulated in the light of biblical and new historical-contextual elements.

Paradoxically, Catholicism (which Adventism harshly criticizes) seems to express more important historical and eschatological wisdom. Catholic eschatology is a typical postmillennialist eschatology, that is, an optimistic eschatology of the present managed by the church. While pre-Constantinian Catholicism was certainly premillennialist in spirit, post-Constantinian Catholicism (present-day Catholicism) is essentially postmillennialist because the "Constantinian turn" also theologically represents the shift from "suffering with Christ" to "reigning with him."[5] This euphoria in the management of the present through the church has suffered hard blows in recent centuries, but it has not changed essentially. It has simply shifted from a political dimension to an ethical–social dimension.

Catholicism has not been idle. It has learned from its mistakes. It has developed one of the most innovative, consistent, and penetrating critiques of modern secular postmillennialist euphoria from its classic religious postmillennialist vantage point. Most striking is that Catholicism's critique of the present was made at the end of the nineteenth century when modernity was ascendant, when it was impossible to foresee the contradictions

---

5. This is, for example, Jürgen Moltmann's description of Catholicism. See Moltmann, *Coming God*, 150–56.

and alienations that secular modern postmillenarianism would bring. This Catholic critique was embodied and articulated in the "social thought of the church," born with Leo XIII's *Rerum Novarum* (May 1891). *Rerum Novarum* is a concentrate of reflections and criticism of modern capitalism, starting with its perverse effects on the working class. It is also a critique of the nascent socialist solution to target civil society by betting on intermediate bodies and associations.

Three years after Adventism delivered its harsh premillennialist critique of the present (in a spiritual tone) through the reformulating of *The Great Controversy* in 1888 (second edition), in 1891, sociocultural Catholicism produced a broader, more consistent, and more visionary postmillennialist critique of the present through *Rerum Novarum*. And while Catholicism has continued to revive, update, complete, and modulate that already tough, incisive, even rash critique of the present (including Pius XI's *Quadragesimo Anno* (1931), Paul VI's *Octogesima Adveniens* (1971), and especially John Paul II's *Centesimus Annus* (1991)), Adventism's premillennialist critique in *The Great Controversy* not only has become anachronistic, its analysis is stuck in the nineteenth century. More importantly, Adventism has confined its critique to the spiritual realm without any serious consideration of cultural, economic, or political dimensions of present history.

Apocalyptic obsession creates inflexibility that impoverishes our eschatological proposals by making them compulsive and unresponsive; militant, not dialogical; static, not dynamic; and exclusionary, not inclusive. Apocalyptic militancy, once Adventism's ally, has become its enemy because it magnifies insignificant things and diminishes things of greatest importance. Postapocalyptic Adventism could enable the reordering of our priorities, teaching us to give space and expression to the things that matter most. In the process, we may find that the center of eschatology is not the Adventist church but others—and God's broad and deep regard for the world and all its inhabitants. God's kingdom incarnated in the "common good" is a reality that goes beyond any particular confession.

14

Praise of Laodicea

The idea of praising lukewarmness in this day and age is not only laughable, it seems deliberately, even childishly, provocative. This is a time of boldness, a time of decisiveness. With the new US presidential administration currently creating economic and social chaos at home and abroad, the political theory of decisionism is manifest. This president-*über-alles* leadership model values clarity and efficiency in decision-making without delay or hesitation. It does not get lost in law, history, dialogue, or reflection but cavalierly sets a crystal clear course.

In his book *In Praise of Meekness*, Italian philosopher of law and political theory Norberto Bobbio identifies this humble virtue as one of the most important values for our time. Bobbio writes,

> I love meek people because they are the ones who make this "flowerbed" more habitable, so much so that it makes me think that the ideal city is not the one fantasized and described down to the minutest detail by utopians but one in which kindness of customs has become a universal practice.[1]

Meekness should not be confused with submissiveness or passivity. It is at once a weak virtue—befitting those who exercise no power—and a powerful one, since it anticipates a better world and envisions a different

---

1. Bobbio, *Elogio della mitezza*, 13.

future. It is "the most apolitical of virtues," says Bobbio.[2] It is also an antidote to civic degeneration that has resulted in today's political etiquette of swagger and obscene in-your-face demeanor, devoid of modesty or self-reflection.

But meekness is not merely a politicoethical value. It is also a cultural remedy against what Israeli intellectual Amos Oz calls the drift into fanaticism. In his 2015 book *Against Fanaticism*, a collection of three lectures delivered in Tübingen, Germany, in 2002, Oz reminds us that political decisionism, the cult of immediate and non-negotiated decision-making, is both the antechamber and natural extension of fanaticism in all its forms.[3]

The growing example of decisionism in the US is rooted deeply in that culture. In the early nineteenth century, Alexis de Tocqueville noted this combination of great virtues and great anomalies in American democracy.[4] Birthed in the political tensions that inspired Tocqueville's study, Adventism is not immune from this decisionist drift. In some ways, it even anticipates it. The Adventism of the past two decades might be the most decisionist in its history because of its mix of extreme presidential power and its emphasis on an excessively homogeneous religious community. The theological homogeneity typical of Adventism since its inception was—in the past—tempered by institutional pluralism, with checks and balances at various organizational levels. Much of that has disappeared today. Adventism is becoming an embodiment of the purely political decisionism that currently rages through reactionary societies.

LAODICEA: LUKEWARMNESS VS. MODERATION

In this religiopolitical context, it is worth pausing to consider the associations that define the church of Laodicea. Presented prophetically as the last of the seven churches in the book of the Apocalypse, it has become synonymous with disengagement, indifference, and spiritual torpor. In a word, its fault and sin would be that of being "lukewarm." The political and religious decisionism represented thus far could be read as an attempt at escaping from cultural lukewarmness. But is authority the antidote to apathy? Any serious diagnosis must try to articulate a differential diagnosis.

2. Bobbio, *Elogio della mitezza*, 19.
3. Oz, *Contro il fanatismo*, 12–13.
4. De Tocqueville, *Democracy in America*, 571–690.

Following this track, while opposite, lukewarmness and decisionism would be two sides of the same coin. Decisionism often embodies the desire to correct a laissez-faire drift that has become chronic, just as lukewarmness not infrequently takes over to cool a red-hot will to power. But the most important question about Laodicea concerns its essence. Is Laodicea lukewarm, lazy, and indifferent by nature, or does something even more essential lie behind these attitudes? To put it in a word, it seems that the essence of Laodicea is "moderation"—the capacity of being equidistant from hot or cold. Laodicea embodies the wisdom of avoiding extremes; it demonstrates the ability to know how to be balanced.

We should therefore avoid diminishing Laodicea, as sometimes happens with difficult children, by trying to correct Laodicea's faults. Laodicea is certainly sick with lukewarmness, but its lukewarmness is the deformation of a virtue—in this case, the virtue of moderation. So, against lukewarmness and against decisionism, one must enforce the value of moderation, temperance, and the rejection of radicalism. The essence of Laodicea in times of civic and religious radical forms is learning to cultivate a sense of measure in the presence of ideologically overheated and reckless militancy. This is the lesson we should learn from Laodicea.

The seven churches in Revelation (Rev 1:12–19) each have a unique profile, and none of them embodies the fullness of Christ. Each is only a part. We see this in the contrast between the church in Ephesus and the church in Laodicea. Most readings mistakenly favor Ephesus over Laodicea as the ecclesial prototype to be imitated, but one cannot asymmetrically compare the virtues of one entity with addressing the faults of another.

The church in Ephesus is certainly a militant church, characterized by full love. This is a good thing; but it also embodies possibly devastating excess. One eventual problem of the church of Ephesus is, paradoxically, a love that becomes too compact and intransigent. Lukewarmness seems to define Laodicea, but there is a time and place for everything. Sometimes moderation in spiritual matters is good, as with water temperature. Laodicea is not asked to become Ephesus. But inspired by Ephesus, Laodicea offers the contrast of moderation.

MODERATE EUROPEAN ADVENTISM

Europe is a geopolitical symbol of the capacity to be equidistant—moderate, even more than the United States. Developments of the last several months demonstrate this. Modern Europe was born under the sign of religious moderation—the Peace of Westphalia in 1648—that ended the Thirty Years' War and was produced by the religious excess of Catholics *and* Protestants. Although imperfect, this spirit urgently needs to be rediscovered in the face of the religiopolitical unilateral and decisionist thrusts that characterize these days.

This is where European Adventism has something to offer. Its voice is vitally important in the pluralistic context of world Adventism. There is no one Adventism. European Adventism, precisely because it is European, is a moderate Adventism. It is typically a Laodicean Adventism in the best sense—knowing how to be measured and dialogical.

THE GREAT CONTROVERSY VERSUS *STEPS TO CHRIST* IN ITALY

Here is a brief historical example: last year, Italian Adventism celebrated its 160th anniversary. It was in the Waldensian valleys of the Italian Piedmont that the first European Adventist, Catherine Revel, was baptized in 1864. It was a convinced Adventism, full of passion for the Bible and Christ's second coming. By then, it was already a European Adventism—a moderate Adventism.

When E. G. White's book *The Great Controversy* was first printed in the United States in 1858; more than sixty years would pass before its publication in Italian, which did not occur until 1926. *The Great Controversy* is a militant book, not a moderate one. While decisionist Adventism considers it the sole and highest expression of the Adventist metanarrative, European Adventism has processed it with difficulty. While appreciating it, European Adventism harbors some perplexity and doubt.

Different is the fate and history of the book *Step to Christ* in Italy. The book was published in the United States in 1892. It appeared in Italian immediately two years later in 1894, printed by the Waldensians in their publishing house, La Claudiana, which is still active.

The bid for a moderate Adventism in Italy and Western Europe, characterized, for example, by this book, is present from the very beginning. It is also evident in the work of the best-known American Adventist missionary in Italy in the early twentieth century, Charles Everson. He would found a community in Rome between 1902–1909, marked by this religious moderation of respect and dialogue inherent to the Italian culture of the time.

Part II: Vulnerability and Flourishing

CAREFUL, COURAGEOUS ADVENTISM

Certainly moderation as a cultural and religious form does not appear only with Laodicea. It is also typical of classical Greek culture, which saw the harmony of the laws of the cosmos as a sphere not to be exceeded. This will be the sin imputed to Prometheus, for example. Nietzsche, in his book *The Birth of Tragedy*, will be critical of this restraint and will stigmatize it as a cultural defect.[5] In this same vein, the middle way is also typical of the ethical thinking of Aristotle and incarnated in his "golden mean."[6] Virtue is always a middle way. Courage, in fact, is neither recklessness nor being cowardly but the clear affirmation of a will and action that remain nevertheless sober and not overbearing. German philosopher Peter Sloterdijk gives an esthetical and philosophical interpretation of the virtue of moderation through the valorization of a stigmatized color: gray. A luminous trace of many everyday situations, gray is the symbol of a healthy indifference, writes Sloterdijk, that urges us to lay down the weapons of continuous struggle, to choose an "active mediumness" at the service of a greater event.[7] Thus is affirmed a new aesthetic and philosophical theory of compromise between light and dark.

This perspective of moderation is also present in the Bible's wisdom literature. Wisdom (*chokmah*) is the art of human and religious sobriety. Laodicea, then, against all appearances, embodies a great virtue worth valuing today in the face of rampant, self-justifying, and short-sighted decision-making. For various reasons, not always easy to analyze, this religious moderation appears to global Adventism as a capitulation of faith that must be avoided at all costs. This moderate Adventism is certainly slower theologically and administratively. But this carefulness is urgently needed in Adventism. It is not graduality resulting from laziness or disengagement but an ethos grounded in the pauses necessary for dialogue and to hear the knocking at the door of events, persons, and history.

---

5. Nietzsche, *Birth of Tragedy*.
6. Aristotle, *Nicomachean Ethics*.
7. Sloterdijk, *Grigio*, 12–13.

15

The Value of a Kenotic Adventism

WE USUALLY BELIEVE THAT in order to survive, we need to affirm ourselves, even to the point of defending our cultural or religious identity with extreme coherence, conviction, and zeal against all who represent a threat, through a necessary and justified struggle for survival. This antagonist model has been contested in various ways and at various levels as being a short-sighted and biased model. This critique emerged within the theory of evolution itself, where Darwin and the first Darwinians saw life as a necessary struggle for survival against threatening species. Biologist Lynn Margulis, citing recent discoveries in biology, points out that in order to survive, we need to cooperate with other species rather than fight against them.[1] To have allies, not enemies, is what true life is really all about, adds Dona Haraway, in what she calls the art of "making kin not population."[2] Cooperating with other biological entities means, essentially, the implicit acceptance of my own species' incompleteness and, at the same time, acknowledging the value of other species for my own survival. Neither "hetero-poiesis," a total dependence from the outside world, nor "auto-poiesis," a linear understanding of an exclusive self-affirmation, but rather "sym-poiesis," adds Haraway, understood as a cooperative and relational life affirmation.

1. Margulis, *Symbiotic Planet*, 6–19.
2. Haraway, *Making Kin Not Population*, 79–118.

Part II: Vulnerability and Flourishing

This is what kenotic identity means: incompleteness and cooperation. As Italian philosopher Leonardo Caffo says, ours is a "fragile humanity."[3] This is not a disadvantage but rather an asset in a relational understanding of life, that is necessarily a hetero-oriented life by making others part of my own. Italian philosopher of science Emanuele Coccia speaks about "cosmic twinship," or "cosmic consanguinity," in the sense that every birth is a "twin birth," in which the world and subjects are heterozygous twins—diverse but united, born at the same time and unable to define oneself without the other.[4] Birth is not only an event of differentiation and separation but also a movement of convergence and assimilation.

According to French-North African philosopher Pierre Zaoui in *The Art of Disappearing*, we have to learn to understand this relational perspective that describes the primordial mechanism of true life.[5] Only when we live with discretion, wisely combining affirmation and recognition of others, can we aspire to true happiness.[6] This is the essence of a kenotic life: a life that doesn't give up passion for life but rather affirms it by linking it to the survival of others, because only as others survive is our own survival possible.

Every identity, individual, or group struggles between the need to affirm itself and the parallel need to allow other identities around us to affirm themselves through our recognition. If, to affirm ourselves, we need "conviction," we need "flexibility" to allow others to affirm. The problem lies in the fact that keeping "conviction" and "flexibility" together is not at all obvious or automatic. It is like wanting to accelerate and brake at the same time. Linear machines cannot do that. Humans, on the other hand, can, albeit with effort and only through a slow process of learning and maturing. This is a sign and proof of our humanity. And what is valid for life in general is also valid for faith. Faith cannot be reduced to a linear experience of pure militancy.

Often, religion, instead of contributing to the proper and wise maintenance and management of this human paradox, goes out of its way to dismantle it. In doing so, our faith ends up deformed. The identities that erase this paradox emerge impoverished, even if this impoverishment is frequently covered by increased functionality and efficiency that makes proper diagnosis difficult.

---

3. Caffo, *Fragile umanità*, 5–18.
4. Coccia, *Matamorfosi*, 26–28.
5. Zaoui, *Arte di scomparire*, 8–21.
6. Zaoui, *Arte di essere felici*, 21–34.

The Value of a Kenotic Adventism

The health of an identity cannot be reduced to one or the other of these two elements, "conviction" or "flexibility." These elements introduce a structural tension with which one must learn to live. Maintaining this tension becomes evidence and sign of having reached maturity of life and faith. This urge, not to impoverish life and faith, comes not only from God but also from life itself, according to Olivier Roy in his book *The Flattening of the World*.[7]

This is what we have tried to describe in this series on Adventism (Ecclesiological Holzwege): "A Reasonable Adventism," "A Slow Adventism," "A Post-Apocalyptic Adventism," "A Post-Whitean Adventism," etc. Mainline Adventism should be credited with the value of the constant call to faithful militancy without ifs and buts. But behind this call lies a possible danger that must never be lost sight of in the euphoria of faith. This danger is the unilateralism of a faith that becomes effective but at the same time loses the value of complexity. Without complexity, faith, without realizing it, becomes a superficial faith and is consequently less resilient.

We have, from various sociological and cultural perspectives and various authors, called for the urgent need that Adventism not lose sight of complexity in the euphoria of a compactly militant Adventism. The step is short from compact militancy to religious, missionary, ethical, or apocalyptic fanaticism. When one gets there, the call for moderation becomes almost impossible because it is automatically perceived as a dangerous temptation that diverts us from faith and is therefore to be avoided.

In the search for this complexity, we have tried to value a minority type of Adventism, one that is a resource for the world church: European Adventism. We have considered European Adventism as an "ideal type," in Max Weber's sense, not necessarily in the realization of all those perspectives and seeds it carries. The realization of a faith community, beyond numbers and appearances, is as difficult everywhere in Europe as it is in Africa or Latin America.

All of this is articulated and revolves around what we might call the need for a "kenotic Adventism." Not a muscular Adventism, much less an overbearing or reckless one, this "kenotic Adventism" erases neither convictions nor militancy, and less, still, a passion for the gospel and mission. It simply gives a needed dimension of sobriety (for us) and greater empathy (with others) in the face of a life and faith that have become, perhaps more than any other time, complex and heterogeneous realities.

7. Roy, *Appiattimento del mondo*.

Part II: Vulnerability and Flourishing

Discovering the value of a "kenotic religion" implies reappropriating an attitude that has been somewhat lost today—that of "vulnerability." Vulnerability is more resilient than compact and linear strength. Vulnerability is not an "ethical virtue" but a "relational virtue" that presupposes one's own incompleteness and sincere appreciation of the other. The other is not necessarily an enemy, just as we are never fully self-sufficient. Here are the essential data of what an "anthropology of vulnerability" is and represents in its connection to a "kenotic" faith.

The presence of others always introduces an element of confusion, opacity, and disorder that prevents a perfect theological or social order. Others, whether individuals, peoples, or other species, always slow our pace and act as disturbing elements and obstacles precisely through the incommensurability and opacity of their mystery. Recovering an anthropology of vulnerability is essential, not only in a human key but also in a theological and hermeneutical key, because it is from humanity's arrogance that the arrogance of its texts derives. The arrogance of a faith community inevitably corresponds with the arrogance of its sacred texts. Only an anthropology of vulnerability is able to give birth to a vulnerable hermeneutics. In "kenotic hermeneutics," the bearer of a flexible and welcoming meaning opposes the presumption of a biblical rigidity that sometimes remains among us after we overcome an inerrant view of the Bible.

This is the call of Bernhard Waldenfels in his *Phenomenology of the Other*.[8] The central feature of this discovery of the Other, according to Waldenfels, is not the relevance of our question so much as the vulnerability of our response. Our word is never primary and therefore is not initially configured as a question but as a response to a voice there before us, one that precedes us and challenges us.[9] When the Other resumes its place, we regain our vulnerability, the foundation of a possible relationality. Relationality is never the certainty of the Self over the Other but the reliance on the Other over a vulnerable self. Such vulnerability does not make life more precarious; it rather makes it full through the non-manipulation of the Other, who thus always remains a "stranger," not a threat but a source of "extraordinariness." Thus, the Other as "stranger" (*straneo*), as "foreign"

---

8. Waldenfels, *Studien zur Phänomenologie*. See particularly, Waldenfels, *Topographie des Fremdes*, 16–53.

9. Waldenfels, *Grundmotive einer Phänomenologie*, 56–67.

(*estraniero*), and as "extraordinariness" (*straordinario*) determines the cornerstones of an anthropology of vulnerability.[10]

This vulnerability as a relational experience in the face of the other, the basis of a "kenotic Adventism," implies two essential attitudes as a precondition. First, "af-fect" (affection), which is not the capacity to feel something but rather the capacity to welcome and be affected, to be touched by what comes to us from outside. From being numb to the voices of others, from the muteness of things and people that we had turned into manipulatable and dumb objects, we instead become, for the first time, capable of being touched by voices that we stop manipulating. Affection is the afferent pathway from the outside coming to us, creating a feeling that we do not produce, but simply the effect of others that reaches us. The world is no longer indifferent; it speaks to us.

Second, "e-motion," which is not the ability to feel something but rather the momentum that starts from us toward others after we have been resurrected by the voice of others. "E-motion" is the centrifugal movement that allows us for the first time, precisely because we are alive, to offer something of ourselves to others. Emotion is the efferent way from us to others by transmitting life. We are no longer indifferent to this external world; we are able to give something—our voice and our testimony.

We conclude with a historical reference to a work of art built around a kenotic God. *The Last Judgment*, painted by Giorgio Vasari in the dome of Florence Cathedral, is the world's only artistic representation of *Apokatastasis ton Panton* (God's Universal Salvation). Having in mind Michelangelo's unsurpassed work *The Last Judgment* in Rome's Sistine Chapel, Vasari wonders if the word "judgment" could be the last word of a God of mercy. Michelangelo's *Last Judgment*, well known to us all, represents well what we all mean by judgment. Judgment is verification, distinction, separation, an unequivocal and unappealable final verdict.

Vasari wanted to make a better painting than Michelangelo's, not in an artistic sense but in a theological one. He knew that Michelangelo was unsurpassed artistically. He was criticized for this apparent presumption. He talked to Vincenzo Borghini, a philosopher and refined philologist of the Italian Renaissance, regarded as one of the most learned people of that period. He asked the question that had been running through his head day and night: can judgment be the last word of a merciful God? Borghini

---

10. Waldenfels, *Estraneo, straniero, straordinario*, 13–36.

spoke to him about *Apokatastasis ton Panton*, God's universal salvation.[11] Origen has surfaced here and there in the minds of some theologians but had always been declared a heretic. What is seen in Michelangelo's painting as divided, separate, distinct, the fate of the good and evil, Vasari's work imagines them together, encompassed by the glory of God. Vasari did not give an answer but he certainly asked a good question.

I, too, have doubts about *Apokatastasis ton Panton* as a theological answer. I nevertheless welcome it not only as a legitimate question but a necessary one. Can the final judgment unfold as we Adventists represent it in our sometimes radical and extreme apocalypticism? Can we know in detail how this judgment will unfold, and what outcomes it will have? It would be heterodox to exclude judgment as God's final act, but it is equally anomalous to think that we can describe it in a linear and unambiguous way. God will certainly judge. But he will certainly not be as we imagine him. He will be something more than an implacable judge. We must not say more than what is written, and we must always remain sober. Here are the extremes of a kenotic Adventism that does not give up its certainties but it says them soberly, with empathy, without overbearance and recklessness. A kenotic Adventism avoids giving the impression that it knows more than God himself about faith, life, morals, other churches, judgment, or the future.

---

11. Ramelli, *Christian Doctrine of Apokatastasis*.

16

Rootedness, Inclusiveness and Flourishing

Be like a tree planted by streams.

PSALM 1:3

PSALM 1

I
¹ Blessed is the one
   who does not walk in step with the wicked
or stand in the way that sinners take
   or sit in the company of mockers,
² but whose delight is in the law of the Lord,
   and who meditates on his law day and night.
³ That person is like a tree planted by streams of water,
   which yields its fruit in season
and whose leaf does not wither—
   whatever they do prospers.

PART II: VULNERABILITY AND FLOURISHING

II
⁴ Not so the wicked!
 They are like chaff
 that the wind blows away.
⁵ Therefore the wicked will not stand in the judgment,
 nor sinners in the assembly of the righteous.
⁶ For the Lord watches over the way of the righteous,
 but the way of the wicked leads to destruction.

HERMANN GUNKEL CLASSIFIES THIS psalm as a "wisdom poem."[1] It is divided into two stanzas.[2] The first stanza describes the path of the righteous, who are called "blessed" and are compared with a tree. The emphasis, therefore, is put neither on human discipline nor on moral consistency. The emphasis is rather placed on satisfaction and blessing as conditions and gifts freely received from God that enable the "blessed" to flourish. The second stanza, on the other hand, is a description of the ungodly who are compared with "chaff" that the wind carries away. The emphasis is not on the transgression or recklessness of the ungodly but on their anthropological anonymity and sociocultural inconsistency.

This psalm embodies the perfect model of complexity, not only from the point of view of the form (plural, opposing, and sequential stanzas), that can't be reduced to a single literary element, but also from the point of view of the exposition of contrasting themes (praise and law/individual and community/hymn and lamentation) that can't be absorbed in a final theological synthesis. For this reason, this psalm has been included at the beginning of the Psalter as a kind of thematic introduction and literary model of what comes later in the five books that make up the collection of Psalms. Between hymn, complexity, slowness, wisdom, and flourishing, there is a narrow connection and interdependence, and of this heterogeneous net of categories, this psalm is a persuasive example.

I. "FLOURISHING KIN":[3] WISDOM AND LIFE

Wisdom literature is usually described as an individual, realistic, and critical reflection on life. In the Bible, it is mostly linked to the experience of King

---

1. Gunkel and Begrich, *Einleitung in die Psalmen*.
2. Ravasi, *Salmi*, 29–31; Lancellotti, *Salmi*, 83–86; Mays, *Psalms*, 40–44; Brueggemann and Bellinger, *Psalms*, 27–31.
3. Celidwen, *Flourishing Kin*, 5–21.

Solomon (Ecclesiastes) who, after having lived a life that guaranteed almost unlimited pleasure, as was the power of kings at that time, he stopped in the final period of his life and weighed the merits and demerits, advantages and disadvantages, of the experiences lived. And from this exercise, he drew a kind of minimalist but effective ethics with respect to what really matters in life. Wisdom literature does not begin or end with Solomon, even if, in the Bible, Solomon represents the prototype of this kind of literature. Beyond the schematism that places it in a late period in Solomon's life, we could say, along with Gerhard Von Rad, that wisdom literature basically emerges in the later stages of a group history when that group has the opportunity of reflecting on its own past experiences.[4] Wisdom does not present itself as encouragement to act or live but rather as a reflection on how we have acted and lived. It is, above all, a reflection on the paradox of human action. In this sense, wisdom literature, of which this psalm is an expression, is an indirect affirmation of God through a direct affirmation of life in its essential forms.[5] Its strength consists in making a natural and simple description of life, beyond and before the eventual necessary prescriptions we all need. It is an atypical way of affirming life starting from life itself.[6]

In a world like ours, which has become mechanically and transversally secularized, excessively realistic and cynical about the possibility of "being happy," the rediscovery of biblical and non-biblical wisdom literature represents a healthy breath of fresh air. This is the thesis of social psychologist Jonathan Haidt in his book *The Happiness Hypothesis*, in which he describes the resistance of our happiness-anemic societies to go beyond a functionalist paradigm.[7] Functionality is by no means synonymous with health, even less with happiness.

The common thread that links the various forms of wisdom reflection, biblical and non-biblical, in addition to their critical look of a pure ethical and religious prescriptive paradigm, is found in the connection of spirituality to life, to the group, and to nature. In fact, for the Amerindian peoples, particularly those of the Andes, the highest goal of a life is expressed in the *suma qamaña*[8] (living well) principle. "Living well" is not limited to a so-

---

4. Von Rad, *Weisheit in Israel*.
5. Collins, *Introduction to the Hebrew Bible*.
6. Perdue, *Wisdom and Creation*, 19–48.
7. Haidt, *Happiness Hypothesis*, ix–xiii.
8. Medina, *Suma Qamaña*, 12–32; Mamani, *Vivir bien/Buen vivir*, 33–51; Solon, *¿Es posible el Vivir Bien?*, 8–16.

lipsistic well-being but to living well with others, with nature, and with the divine. In other words, the center of wisdom is bonding and relationships.

German philosopher and biologist Andreas Weber reminds us that, while the West embodies the typical example of cultural involution that has become chronic, which manifests itself precisely in the impossibility of seeing the bond as the foundation of life, actually sees bonds as obstacles to life. On the contrary, cultures of the South see life in the bond. Relationships are the essence of life. Andreas Weber writes,

> Every individual can exist only because his existence is indebted to another. People need parents and a social environment to grow healthy, they need other beings who nourish them, the air, the earth. "I exist because you are here" is more important than the phrase "I am me and you are you." Reality can remain fruitful only if this reciprocity is preserved, if others are sacred, and if what is given to me always gives rise to a gesture of gratitude.[9]

The same idea of wisdom as wisdom in the bond is expressed by Yuria Celidwen in her book *Flourishing Kin*.[10] According to wisdom literature, no spirituality is detached from life, and life is always a related life. As a living experience, every possible flourishing is only possible in the bond. In fact, James L. Mays reminds us that Ps 1, a wisdom psalm par excellence, does not begin with a prayer, a hymn, or a lament but with a declaration of human existence.[11] It is a psalm that praises the Torah, but in a wisdom context and in a wisdom form. We are committed to ideals, principles, or norms only as catalyzing mechanisms for affirming life in its concreteness and immanence.

a. A Wisdom Hymn

Even though Ps 1 is not formally a hymn, it nevertheless conveys the affirmation of life typical of a hymn. The hymnal affirmation in the Psalms embodies three important dimensions of the faith experience.

1. The first dimension is anthropological. The hymn is characterized by gratitude that affirms life and its value despite adverse circumstances. More than a liturgical act or an ethical behavior of resilience, the praise

---

9. Weber, *Indigenialität*, 110.
10. Celidwen, *Flourishing Kin*, 5–21.
11. Mays, *Psalms*, 40–41.

expressed in the hymn articulates and highlights a prerational attitude of trust. This does not mean that in the hymn, words, concepts, and beliefs, dependent on a more rational choice, do not count or count little. All these elements presuppose an awareness and individual commitment and determine it positively. They determine it, in the sense of influencing it, but they do not create it. In this sense, the hymn, more than being a musical or liturgical form, is an anthropological event. In the hymn, this basic anthropological affirmation of life finds its best expression in connecting the individual's personal faith to God. This prerational affirmation of life, which Spinoza called "conatus," is not only expressed in liturgical music or in religious communities. This universal anthropological event is transversal to all humanity. The hymn is an anthropological event and expression of the desire to live a life able to desire relations. The relationship between "hymn" and "conatus" is therefore a close and natural relationship that does not take away the specificity of the liturgical form of the hymn but, on the contrary, clarifies its essence. Will, memory, reason, conviction, commitment, or decision come after, not before this vital affirmation. They simply presuppose or prolong it through useful and concrete rituals.

2. The second dimension of the hymn is psychological. The hymn is linked to the psychological truth of the subject. As such, it does not ask how things really happened, or what really is their historical or sociological objectivity. The hymn asks, how do things happen to me? The hymn is a psychological event expressing the subjective truth that is born in the subject and in his specific experience. It is perception, not of the objective event but of its impact on the psyche of the subject—in this case, the worshiper. The force of revealed truth or of sacred data tends to minimize, sometimes even delegitimize, the validity of this psychological truth. Individuals, if recognized as such, must also be recognized as having the right to perceive objective data according to their own subjective sensitivity. The hymn is not the revealed Word of God but is the subjective perception and response to that word that individuals express according to their own context sensitivity. In this sense, the hymn articulates the concrete right to be, for single worshipers, an anthropological legitimate actor.

3. The third is a cultural dimension. Praise and music in premodern cultures, such as those of the Old or New Testaments, expressed a *sui generis* way of being in the world. They were transitive experiences that put people in contact, not only with each other but also with God and with nature. They were relational events in which people linked themselves to life and

live life as a relational event characterized by trust and joy. According to Erich Fromm, these were typical communities of instinctive communitarian joy (orgiastic communities) and typical communities of balance.[12] These communities, which we moderns call primitive and indolent because they were "slow communities," placed pleasure, music, and praise at the center of their lives. Our so-called "civilized societies" have instead introduced a cultural revolution that consists in choosing organized work as the engine of their growth, reaching unimaginable goals of well-being and efficiency. In so doing, they have been forced to make pleasure, music, and praise emigrate to the periphery of life. We probably make more music today but it's no longer at the center of life. Civilization has extinguished the *eros* that is at the basis of the joy of living, typical of the hymnal form. We exchange joy for satisfaction and exuberance for responsibility. The goal of life is work and ethical reliability, not free singing. Those who sing and affirm life as the hymnal form does are considered atypical, eccentric, and, necessarily, lazy. Civilized persons are composed and measured, always busy achieving their own projects by controlling their feelings and the excesses of their instinctive lives. Music and praise, no longer at the center of life, lose their relational character, made of the discovery and desire of the other. They become, instead, experiences of individual leisure and personal amusement and gratification. Our performance societies no longer know how to sing and praise because they do it as a parenthesis of life, no longer at its center. We sing and dance to enhance and guarantee more efficient work, not to limit it, much less to transform it. We, performative and disciplined workers, do not live in music but of music. We manipulate it according to our production goals and strategies.

b. A Wisdom Anthropology

In Ps 1, a double anthropological outlook is articulated in connection with the two stanzas that comprise this poem: on one hand, we find the anthropology of the righteous, those characterized by the capacity of resisting sin and temptation, and, on the other, the anthropology of the wicked, characterized here not by their vocation to transgression but by their inconsistency and strong self-destructive drive. A proper reading of this psalm thus tries to keep these two anthropological levels in tension.

---

12. Fromm, *Art of Loving*, 15–24.

But this psalm also introduces an element external to humanity, creating a second tension. This is the introduction of an ecological element, which reminds us that ethics is not only about internal coherence but also about external correspondence, i.e., about social and ecological correspondence. It proposes an anthropological model from an ecological perspective. In other words, before humanity, we find nature. Nature is the necessary background to understand correctly what is human, its essence and vocation. This ecological-human description principle and determinant is not autonomy but relation, not awareness but prerational intentionality, not perseverance and determination but trust and flourishing, understood as the reception of a beauty we are unable to create ourselves but that arrives by grace, coming from God and others.

This psalm is structurally very clear and symmetrical. It has two parts—two stanzas that are quite distinct and discernible. For this reason, it has always been read as the psalm "of the two ways." On the one hand, the way of the righteous: the blessed one who obeys God's law (verses 1–3); and on the other, the way of the wicked who, by opposing God, easily lose consistency, becoming like chaff carried away by the wind (verses 4–6). My hypothesis is that this classical reading is correct, provided it is complemented by a second reading that introduces into the text a less visible, less immediate, but more decisive rupture in the overall meaning of the psalm. This ecological element is introduced in verse 3: the tree. This more hidden dimension of the psalm proposes as more determinant not the differentiation between the righteous and the corrupt, between good and bad, between believers and unbelievers, but the differentiation between "the one who walks" (verses 1, 2) and "the one who does not walk" (verse 3). We find this differentiation not by comparing the first and second stanzas but within the first stanza.

So, we could call this psalm not the psalm "of the two ways" but the psalm of the "two lives." In other words, being able to distinguish right from wrong is the first step in faith. But it is not enough. This step is only the first step, necessary but insufficient. The second step is to know whether we are passing on "life" or, rather, "death." Not right or wrong, not truth or falsehood, not consistency or inconsistency—all essential but insufficient criteria to describe what really counts in this human wandering—but "life" lived and transmitted, as opposed to symbolic and metaphorical "death" that stops and imprisons life, even with positive elements such as virtues or truth. This is what is essential in the message of this psalm. To convey life, one must stand still, like the plant that must stand still in order to flourish. This psalm exemplifies and describes the necessary and beneficial transition from ethics to anthropology, from acting to flourishing. Blessed, then, are not those who act correctly but those who flourish and, by flourishing, pass on life to the world and to others.

c. A Wisdom Philosophy

Wisdom literature, like this wisdom hymn, reminds us that the essence of every religious form is connection to life. This life is also expressed in specific forms of a doctrinal, ethical, or ritualistic nature, but these forms are easily deformed when they are disconnected from life. As Arthur Walker-Jones reminds us, the merit of wisdom literature is that of bringing back, or bringing forth, our religious experience to a direct contact with humanity, which is essentially an expression of life.[13] The reference to the law or to holiness, present in this psalm, must therefore be read in function of life and not the opposite. The well-known Italian jurist Stefano Rodotà, in his book *Life and the Norms*, applies this wisdom reading also to today's legal systems, saying that a community (nation, state, etc.) cannot work without a set of rules, whether constitutional or operational.[14] This necessary set of rules gives them a certain order and regularity, making common life possible. And yet, Rodotà adds, those laws and norms are not a final goal. They are rather tools at the service of life that will always have a surplus of meaning compared to the norms that try to regulate it. A legal system, in a wisdom perspective, remains secondary. As such, it must provide for an overcoming of life in relation to the norms that it wants to guarantee. This is what Ps 1 and the philosophy behind it do. This philosophy of life is not antinomian. Indeed, it requires and promotes the existence of a law (Torah) that, at the same time, does not exhaust the richness of life to which it is connected with the intent to regulate it and give it a certain order and predictability.

Contrary to Walter Brueggemann, who classifies this psalm as a psalm of "orientation" by virtue of its strong reference to the Torah,[15] especially in verse 2; we believe that the center of the psalm is verse 3, with the metaphor of the tree. This fact allows us to describe this psalm as a psalm of disorientation

---

13. Walker-Jones, *Green Psalter*, 26–27.
14. Rodotà, *Vita e le regole*, 12–25.
15. Brueggemann, *Message of the Psalms*, 38–39.

because of the strong reference to the unavailability of life perceived precisely as flourishing. If flourishing were a calculation, or only planning, it would no longer flourish at all. The affirmation of life in a typical wisdom perspective, which, in this psalm, opens with the word *asher* (blessed/happy), does not refer to the clarity and predictability of the experience of faith but rather to its incommensurability as flourishing. Those are blessed when they know how to live in the tension of not possessing life and in the awareness of not being able to plan it. Blessed are those who have hope and trust that the fruit for which they have committed themselves, and for which they have worked, will exceed their own planning, efforts, and forecasts.

In psalms like this, we move to the "descriptive mode" from the "declarative mode," says Claus Westermann,[16] freeing the Torah from that prescriptive reading that tends to make life excessively ordered and predictable, thus making it lose its typical "unavailability." The "declarative" mode of any speech mode tends to presuppose a static reality that we can explain and determine with some kind of historical or religious scheme. Life will always be unsettling for any category used to grasp it. Life is life when it is ordered and when that order does not suffocate it. The emphasis on the immanent value of life, typical of wisdom philosophy and theology, is not, as is often believed, to make it more mechanical and predictable by detaching it from God. If anything, it is rather the opposite. The essence of transcendence often makes life mechanical by shifting the value of life to something that transcends it, so disavowing an internal value of its own, as happens in every type of dualism. This valorization of life as a relatively autonomous one, with its own internal value that materializes in flourishing, presupposes two movements that are at the basis of wisdom, philosophy, and theology.

The first movement is the kenosis of God himself. Wisdom literature presupposes a different concept of God by which God is conceived, not in his strength but in his flexibility and vulnerability—something like a present God behind the scenes. If God remained, as in the Torah and in the Prophets, the protagonist and heroic God of the patriarchs, there would be no suitable space for human flourishing. A strong presence of God would hinder and intimidate the full flourishing of humanity. It doesn't mean that God disappears. It only means that God dresses himself in a supporting, facilitating, and mediating role, as a facilitator of humanity's creative action. This is the reason Leo G. Perdue recalls that wisdom literature is linked to

---

16. Westermann, *Praise and Lament*, 117–19.

creation rather than to salvation (transcendent) as a way of valuing creatures.[17] Wisdom theology actually proposes a kenotic version of the Creator.

Creation is therefore an act of "sobriety" through which the Creator renounces the fullness of his prerogatives to give real and concrete space to his creatures. Creation fundamentally presents itself, for all intents and purposes, not as an act of power but as an act of humility. It is a true kenotic act.[18] Kenosis is not only a christological act and does not only have Christ as its protagonist.

Moreover, this is the reading that Isaac Luria made of creation, which is known as the doctrine of Zimzum,[19] a Hebrew term that means precisely the "concentration," "contraction," "withdrawal" of God, in an attitude of humility and kenosis, to truly interact with humanity within the context of the alliance. Gershom Scholem took this concept in Isaac Luria's version and elevated it to one of the fundamental concepts of Judaism.[20] He uses this kenotic version of creation[21] as a correction of the Jewish rational doctrine of the Middle Ages, expressed, for example, in the twelfth century by Maimonides.[22]

This kenotic version of the Creator is represented in Ps 1, which implies that the precondition of human flourishing is the kenosis of God. In alluding to God as water/a stream that nourishes the tree, we find a kenotic description of God. The protagonist in verse 3 is not the water (God) but the tree (humanity). God does not disappear. He is always there but as a minor character, as if in the shadow, as a condition of life for others.

God works behind the scenes as a non-protagonist guarantor so that humanity can flourish. If God always occupies the whole scene, not only would he become a cumbersome and hypertrophic figure, he would paralyze every human initiative. Elliot R. Wolfson speaks about the temptation of what he calls "theomania," which intends to regard God as an always-protagonist God. To limit and avoid that theological drift, Wolfson suggests we need a theological "apophasis," i.e., a kenotic theology of God's

---

17. Perdue, *Wisdom and Creation*, 19–48.

18. From the Greek word κένωσις, which means "to empty oneself, to strip oneself." The most representative verse of kenosis is Phil 2:7, in which "emptying" (lowering) is applied to Jesus in his incarnation: "But he emptied (*ekenosen*) himself, taking the form of a servant, being born in the likeness of men."

19. See Moltmann, *Trinità e Regno*, 120–23.

20. Scholem, *Jüdische Mystik*, 285; Scholem, *Schöpfung aus Nichts*, 87–119.

21. Scholem, *Concetti fondamentali dell'ebraismo*, 43–73.

22. Scholem, *Concetti fondamentali dell'ebraismo*, 4, 21.

discretion and circumspection. The possibility of human action depends on God's sobriety—his ability to step aside. In fact, in the description that Ps 1 makes of the "blessed," comparing them to a luxuriant tree, the presence of the Father does not disappear as a guarantor presence but becomes present in the shadows, a presence that withdraws and hides. Psalm 1:3, in fact, says the following:

> He will be like a tree planted by streams of water, that yields its fruit in its season, and whose leaf does not wither; and whatever he does, it will prosper.

While God is mentioned explicitly in verse 2 through the reference to his law, it seems that verse 3 is instead a description of humanity that flourishes. In reality, we find an allusion to God also in verse 3, through the metaphor of God as a stream of water. The Father does not disappear; he is present but does not obstruct. In the scene of the tree, God is a secondary figure, a supporting element that functions in the flourishing of humanity.[23]

This reduction of God (Zim Zum) should not, however, be understood only as a guarantee of human autonomy. In her book *Tsimtsum and Modernity*, Agata Bielik-Robson[24] reminds us that God is not only the guarantor of human autonomy but also the guarantor of human flourishing.[25] God not only preserves life but, above all, promotes life. He promotes life by giving space to human flourishing.

The second movement is the kenosis of humanity itself and of its action. The humanism of flourishing, unlike the individualistic, rational, and voluntarist humanism of modernity, is not a humanism that excludes either groups or nature, much less God. The paradox lies in the fact that, while privileging humanity, not in its absolute autonomy but in its relationality, humans and nonhumans come out reassessed and reappraised. Making flourishing central means renouncing the strong anthropological model of control of the sovereign self. The category of flourishing opposes and contrasts the anthropology of sovereignty with an anthropology of vulnerability. When we try to be more alone, we end up being alone and less. When we try to be more with others, others are part of our success. Vulnerability, especially in this cultural season that aims at autonomy and at perfect control of human processes, is not a spontaneous or immediate

---

23. Walker-Jones, *Green Psalter*, 28–29.
24. Bielik-Robson, *Tsimtsum and Modernity*.
25. See also Bielik-Robson, *Another Finitude*.

experience. The sovereign self, because it is intelligent and well-informed, feels that it cannot control everything. It, therefore, tends to delegate a part of its prerogatives in order to show itself more flexible, but not to the point of fully surrendering and trusting others. In other words, the sovereign self controls everything that matters for the important levels of human life. For this reason, Elena Pulcini writes that a real *"paideia"* (education) to vulnerability is needed.[26] And that requires time, patience, and flexibility.

An even more important reason that pushes the sovereign self, even without knowing it, to want control of situations and prevents it from seeing vulnerability as a possible ally is its uprooting. The sovereign self's uprooting is ambivalent. On the one hand, it gives him freedom, but on the other hand, it takes away stability. More uprooting brings more desire for control. The sovereign self has been able to control everything precisely because it has disconnected itself from that everything, thus acquiring, as never before, an unlimited freedom that establishes it as a sovereign self. The problem, however, lies in the fact that the sovereign self that controls everything has feet of clay and is very fragile, precisely because it lacks the true stability only bonds can give. Hence, the hidden compensatory mechanism that pushes it to want to control everything as an unconscious way of attaching itself to the rootedness that it lacks. It finds rootedness in the wrong place, that is, in itself, through a radical decisionism that does nothing but increase its discomfort. Rootedness goes beyond the skills and scope of individuals.

In this new anthropology, relationship and vulnerability go hand in hand. Only the perception of being incomplete (vulnerable) leads us to glimpse in relationships a possibility of life and redemption. Individuality, though, is not sacrificed. Autonomy is essential to validate the real strength and existence of everyone. Without autonomy, individuals would be fake. But for autonomous individuals to survive, that autonomy must become a relational autonomy. Only in relationship is it possible to be truly autonomous. Vulnerability for the relationship and relationship in vulnerability is the human equation of flourishing.

Vulnerable individuals who flourish are essentially kenotic beings like the God who created them. Kenotic beings, vulnerable and incomplete, are not an ethical model nor a procedural strategy to appear more human and less overbearing. Kenotic (vulnerable) beings become the starting point, the center, of a new anthropology of trust. Psalm 1 defines humanity in a

---

26. Pulcini, *Tra cura e giustizia*, 145–77.

transitive, hybrid way, starting from characteristics that are not typical of its own species. Others, humans and nonhumans, can very well be part of humanity's identity without feeling threatened or usurped. Indeed, elements that belong to other systems are part of its specific configuration: trees, fruit, sheep, chickens, etc.[27] This structural vulnerability and incompleteness also implies a degree of imperfection and weariness as being part of any human identity. What is important, Daniel S. Milo says in this anthropology of vulnerability, is to be neither perfect humans nor perfect "in-humans" but "good enough humans."[28]

II. THE FLOURISHING HYPOTHESIS:[29] "HE SHALL BE LIKE A TREE THAT YIELDS ITS FRUIT IN ITS SEASON" (PSALM 1)

Psalm 1 is striking for the various metaphors it uses. Of these, the most evocative and powerful is certainly that of the tree. The metaphor of believers as a tree not only resizes the typical individualistic rationalism on which we are still dependent in the development of a Christian ethics but proposes an alternative, by thinking differently to correct and improve it. The psalm indirectly criticizes rationalistic individualism through the figure of the tree by making individuals more anonymous, less apprehensive, and less compulsive. In fact, responsibility, attention, and action from precious virtues have become insidious deformations we need to perceive and correct. The correction of these typical modern deformations doesn't make us stronger, invulnerable, and more resistant. The flourishing as the outcome of the tree's vocation, because it's a relational event, makes the tree vulnerable and fragile.[30] Human goodness, as much as religious goodness, can't be absolute and detached. Becoming absolute is the origin of their perversion. Virtues die not necessarily because of opposed and parallel vices but rather by their own unilateralism and radicalization. The greatness of human and religious goodness, as a reference point of life, faith, and ethics, resides in vulnerability and fragility,[31] in their unconditional availability for relationship and dialogue. Only vulnerable beings can be merciful, relational, and

27. Walker-Jones, *Green Psalter*, 24–25.
28. Milo, *Good Enough*, 1–24.
29. Miller, *Wisdom*, 3–16.
30. Nussbaum, *Fragility of Goodness*, xiii–xxxvii
31. Nussbaum, *Fragility of Goodness*, xiii–xxxvii.

trusting. Not strength but weakness, not fullness but incompleteness, not control but trust, not movement but stillness, not prescription but description, not products but fruits, not mechanisms but people, not goals but purpose, not "futurum" but "adventus," not lines but spheres, not concepts but parables are some correcting categories derived from taking the tree as a metaphor of what humanity should be.

We are, therefore, faced with a true reversal of perspective that we could summarize in these terms: the typical top-down biblical model, which embodies the ideal model of what we are not yet but could be, thanks to divine intervention and our will, here becomes an equally biblical model but of the opposite: a bottom-up model, which starts from validating what there is and how it is what it is. By validating the tree, the goal of believers would no longer be to surpass themselves and become like Paul or Abraham but simply to be themselves, to fulfill their own vocation, their own being. Here, we find the validation of humanity but also humanity as an open and confident event toward flourishing. Flourishing, therefore, expresses a human model that is not voluntarist nor rational, nor individualistic, but relational also in an ecological sense. We confront a model that values humans but does not close them in themselves because it thinks of them as linked and in dialogue with the outside world.

This validation of flourishing shifts the emphasis from individuals to the community, from technique to ecology, and, above all, from "utility" to "goodness." Ethics and the anthropology of "well-being" were common currency in the premodern period until the seventeenth and eighteenth centuries, when the emphasis shifted from the "common good" to "utility." That gave birth, especially in the Anglo-Saxon world (Hobbes, Locke, Smith, Bentham), to a new way of conceiving individuals, their actions, and their humanity. Two or three centuries later, we see now not only the enormously positive aspects of this change, which has created the dynamic and progressive societies we know, but also some collateral effects that have become devastating in some sectors. It is not a question of going back, because that would be impossible, and the intent alone would eventually create more wear, tear, and frustration. The enormous malaise of our time requires correcting, completing, and reworking this valid and innovative Western model in light of a broader perspective that does not stop at the atomism and social and cultural mechanism that grips us.

The first benefit of adopting the model of flourishing, suggested by the psalm, is to put happiness, not functionality, back at the center. The hypothesis of flourishing as a new anthropological and ethical model is, as social psychologist Jonathan Haidt suggests in his book *The Happiness Hypothesis*, a new take on the possibility of being happy.[32] Philosophy, modern science, and modern religion, even without wanting to, have taught us to be efficient and high-performing individuals, making us forget what it means to be happy or even aspire to be so. Self-diagnosis and self-help, understood as self-correcting cultural movements, are not enough. We must learn to look for real alternatives elsewhere. We need to consider non-Western models that have to be contextualized in the West. Because we have unlearned what happiness means, the only way to relearn how to be happy, adds Haidt, is to look "beyond the West," toward non-Western cultures, toward the past that has housed real alternatives to our current model.[33] This is what Haidt undertakes by revisiting and dusting off ancient wisdom, starting from it to relearn how to understand happiness. Other contemporary authors have suggested the same path. Alasdair MacIntyre proposes the revisitation of Aristotle and his ethics of eudaemonia as a way of considering a real alternative.[34] Martha Nussbaum replaces "goodness" at the center of anthropology and ethics, starting with stoicism, especially Greek stoicism.[35] Salvatore Natoli also starts from stoicism, but in its Latin form.[36] We try to do the same but by starting from Ps 1.

"He shall be like a tree that yields its fruit in its season," says the conclusion of the first stanza of the psalm. Flourishing is the goal of a good life, a life guided by God and his Spirit. Let's follow three moments of this first stanza and the description of two types of believers.

a. The Type I believer is the one who walks: "Blessed is the one who does not stop in the way of sinners" (verse 1)

The righteous of the first stanza could be characterized by three traits or virtues that the text suggests are essential in delineating the profile of those who are pious:

---

32. Haidt, *Happiness Hypothesis*, ix–xiii.
33. Haidt, *Happiness Hypothesis*, 105–6.
34. MacIntyre, *After Virtue*.
35. Nussbaum, *Fragility of Goodness*.
36. Natoli, *Felicità*.

a. The ability to avoid evil: "He does not follow the counsel of the wicked" (verse 1)

b. The ability to avoid the wicked: "He doesn't sit in the company of mockers" (verse 1)

c. The ability to walk without becoming distracted: "He does not walk in step with the wicked" (verse 1)

Type I believers are determined: those who have a clear purpose in life, who have no hesitancy or uncertainty concerning the way to follow. They decide, without wavering, to reach the purity and consistency found in God and his Word as an ideal.

This noble Christian lifestyle is certainly admirable and commendable, but it could be short. Walking righteously and diligently is undoubtedly a necessity. But, at the same time, it is insufficient for creating a meaningful life for oneself and others, also because anomalies and vices in the Christian life, unfortunately, do not always emerge in the dark areas of our personality but are often glued to our own virtues and nourished by them.

In fact, walking diligently in the right way can easily become "obsession" and "compulsion" for righteousness. When this happens, righteous living becomes hell, even when formally correct and impeccable. Legitimate caution in the face of evil becomes obsession and paranoia. Avoidance of sitting with the wicked turns into an escape from others because others always embody some kind of deficiency or dysfunction we want to avoid. Walking in faith thus becomes a real compulsion. And this compulsion has a personal as much as a communal version. The personal version is solipsism smuggled in as moral coherence. The communal version is present in many churches when we see in others only enemies, those whom we need to isolate ourselves from, cultivating the false myth of pure faith. The myth of pure faith is idolatry, as was the myth of the pure Aryan race. True faith is always defiled. The guarantor of this is Jesus himself who contaminated his divinity with our humanity. If we want to be with others and for others, we must begin to see contamination with different eyes. Contamination becomes opportunity and does not always represent danger. There is positive contamination and negative contamination. Indeed, healthy contamination with those who are different from us can be a safeguard against ourselves, part of the remedy against our narcissism. Who says that danger comes only from outside, from others? In fact, the greatest danger today comes from within. A religious immunological mechanism risks deforming and destroying us from within, from a hypertrophic us stuck in its own certainties, in its own rituals. Indeed, others, those people different than us, can save us. The maintenance and worship of religious purity leads ineluctably to isolation, implosion, and, finally, to self-destruction. The faith of true believers will not degenerate if they enter into dialogue with Baptists, Waldensians, Roman Catholics, Muslims, or those who are agnostic. Only a faith that has learned to be open, sober, relational, and dialogical is able to survive.

A faith laced with obsessions and paranoia is not virtuous. It does not convey peace and freshness but rather anxiety and unhealthy vertigo. Such a faith needs to be unmasked because it is highly contagious. For that reason, this psalm offers a corrective alternative in opposition to "believers who walk": "believers who don't walk." Those who do not walk are able to flourish like a tree.

b. The Type II believer is the one who does not walk: "He will be like a tree standing still by streams" (verse 3)

Concerning this first model of humans as autonomous beings, who is efficient and in control of the irrational and blind forces in life, this psalm proposes an alternative model: an ecological being in the figure of a tree,[37] which, like nature, instead of control, introduces the metaphor of flourishing as the main metaphor to understand life.

The ecological category underlying this psalm is the tree as a metaphor for what believers are called to be. To the current anthropological model of performativity, efficiency, and all-out production (continuous growth), which presupposes individuals always on the move, in action and in control of their lives and the context in which it takes place, this psalm contrasts the anthropological model of stillness, reliance, and natural and limited production (flourishing) through the motif of a tree.[38] To the typical operational focus and centralization of the classical rational model, the tree model, says Italian biologist Stefano Mancuso, introduces the

---

37. For more on the tree model and its cultural, social, and ethical implications, see chapter 5 of Stefano Mancuso's book entitled "The Intelligence of Plants" in *Verde brillante*, 107–35.

38. But the tree and plants not only introduce a new ethical model of personal and individual management, they also suggest a new model of political management. See Pellegrino, *Etica e politica*, 142–68.

transversality of the network that does not privilege a single command center but entrusts each part of the network with both an operational and ideational dimension.[39] The whole tree thinks, because its intelligence is distributed in each of its parts.[40] The tree model, therefore, is necessarily slower because it has no command center for different functions. But this system makes it more resilient and more operational over time because, even if one part of the tree fails, the essential functions and life of the tree are not at stake. Every part of the tree can survive.

The tree is the prototype of immobile living beings. Here immobility is not thought of as a handicap, as a situation to be overcome, but rather as a resource which guarantees "fullness of life," an embodiment of divine blessing of another order—not according to the order of movement and success but according to the order of immobility and discretion. In this sense, the metaphor of the tree proposes an ideal of life "beyond good and evil," which instead was the narrow and limiting perspective of believers who only walk—not to deny it but to complete it. Type II believers do not grow up with the obsession of having to distinguish between good and evil. They become, above all, witnesses to life against death. The question is no longer how pure we are but rather how much life we are passing on. This dimension is beyond morality, characterized by a full and meaningful existence. It is what Kierkegaard masterfully attributes to Abraham, who, in full trust, throws himself into God's arms, offering him his unique son, his future, beyond reassuring rational and ethical logic.[41] It is the leap of faith. And when faith flourishes, morality is preserved and, at the same time, surpassed. It is preserved in its essence as an open morality, trusting beyond itself in the surplus of life. It is not a paranoid and intimidating fear, incarnated in those who have lost faith in life and are no longer able to flourish, nor are they able to make others flourish.

The tree reaches its life goal not when it avoids sin but when it communicates life through its bud and fruit. Every fruit, like every life, is a miracle, i.e., a transgression. True life, like true love, is always transgressive because it knows how to go beyond what is logical, convenient, what others expect, and what seems possible. So is the life-giving, incommensurate, over-the-top love of a father for a handicapped child, of a pastor for a ruined life, of a doctor for an irreversibly compromised life, of a teacher for a stubborn and

---

39. Mancuso, *Verde brillante*, 32–34.
40. Kohn, *Come pensano le foreste*, 41–77.
41. Kierkegaard, *Fear and Trembling*, 12–34.

unlearning pupil. This love would be impossible if we Christians clung only to the model of mobility. The immobility of life has its own dignity, its own value that a healthy faith must be able to recognize and appreciate. Indeed, this is the antidote this psalm proposes against a compulsive faith obsessed with goals and results.

The value of standing still and unmoving is present across the Bible. It is the virtue of Mary, who listens, versus the busy, almost manic Martha. It is also the focus of the book of Exodus, which, rather than speaking of a people walking and reaching goals, tells us instead of a people who receive God's law (Torah) while still and unmoving. A large section of the Pentateuch, from Exod 18 to Num 10, through all of Leviticus (three books and no less than fifty-nine chapters) tells of a people who are stationary, immobile. In fact, the Hebrew name for the second book of the Bible is not Exodus but *Shemot*, which means "names" in Hebrew. That is, before walking, there must be affirmation and compromise with life, with the essence of who we are in God. Otherwise, walking easily becomes an escape, a compulsion.

c. Flourishing, goal or *telos*? "He shall be like a tree that yields its fruit in its season" (verse 3)

Between the Type I believer who walks and the Type II believer who is stationary, there is no possible alternative. Both are binding. Both are necessary, but the former is propaedeutic to the latter. "Do not evil" is propaedeutic to "flourishing," to doing good. The believers' vocation is to witness life flourishing, not to guard it, and even less to weed a soil where nothing grows. Flourishing is not a goal but rather a purposeful vocation. It is certainly not a goal in the sense that the outcome can't be predicted, organized, or determined in advance. It's rather what Greeks called *telos*, a kind of open direction without determinism, because the outcome always supersedes expectations.

Flourishing, understood as a *telos*, is part of what we could call "spiritual development," as opposed to "religious growth." While "goal" and "growth" are quantitative events, "flourishing" and "spiritual development" are qualitative events. The criteria for "flourishing" as a "spiritual development" are different from those that are valid for "religious growth." "Development" here, essentially, refers to life and life-related events, producing and transmitting life. Characteristics of development are respect for various levels of decision-making: creation and respect for alternative ways within a system; recognition of the mission of other churches and institutions outside of a system; and precisely the degree of fullness and satisfaction given by the metaphor of the tree. Healthy believers, like the tree, have not only increased their size (growth) but, importantly, they have learned to flourish (development).

At this point, the model of the church changes. The goal of the community of faith can no longer be only that of marching onward. The obsessive and mechanical rush toward seemingly religious goals, artificially updated at the cost of detaching ourselves from everyone and everything, easily becomes a mechanical compulsion. The vocation and purpose of believers are to slow down to spend more time with others within our community and also with those outside of it. A tree does not belong only to a particular species of trees but to the entire forest. The tree offers a new model of life and coexistence, the model of balance: balance between the roots that point to the earth and the branches that point to heaven; balance between the leaves that highlight the tree's own beauty, strength, and exuberance; and the fruit that are always for others, never for the tree itself. Through its fruit, the tree says, "The best of me is not meant for myself but for others." Flourishing and the related fruit metaphor introduce a new anthropology and ethics of relationships, of generosity, and of a trusting vulnerability.

This new understanding of the anthropology of flourishing brings also a modification in the understanding of God as the fountain of life. In fact, there is an indirect mention of God in verse 3 through the metaphor of the "water" that allows the tree to grow. The protagonist here is not God but human beings as flourishing trees. But in order for that to happen, God must give up his own protagonism and wear the discreet profile of a supporting God behind the scenes. God, like the water, is presented in Ps 1 as the essential condition for others to live and flourish. God is always there but as a condition (water) that facilitates the life of others.

III. ABORTED FLOURISHING: NECROPHILIAC TEMPTATIONS[42]

"But the way of the wicked leads to death and destruction," says the concluding verse of Ps 1. Is this drive to destruction reserved only for the

---

42. Necrophilia is a rare paraphilia that consists of feeling sexual attraction or performing sexual acts with or in front of a corpse. We will not take this term in this

wicked, or is it more universal and democratic? Does it include also morally reliable people and well-intentioned believers? What drives us to end this chapter, and the entire book, with a negative category? Why describe the force and ambivalent magnetism of necrophilia,[43] privileging it over other more positive categories that emerge in Ps 1? Can our experience of life and personal, family, and community faith take the paradoxical form of a self-destructive drive? Can the expectation of the end become a necrophiliac obsession and can Adventism itself nourish hopelessness? In short, can Adventism become necrophiliac? These questions may surprise and may seem impertinent, ungenerous, even meaningless, especially after having spoken of the experience of flourishing as the one that best embodies the destiny and vocation of those who believe.

Yet, the question of religious and cultural necrophilia is a priority theme that imposes its relevance at the center of the experience of growth and human development. It is closely linked to the theme of flourishing. The "temptation of failing" is real and at hand.[44] In other words, flourishing is not always the happy overcoming of a negative experience that began as erosion, destruction, and depreciation of self. It could also be the opposite. Flourishing often becomes a transitory distraction, an almost preparatory event in a journey that unfortunately ends with cynicism, wear, and tear. In fact, the elderly today do not always express a sense of fullness and satisfaction. Likewise, the faith experiences of adults do not necessarily become inclusive and trusting over time. The shift of attention from the elderly to the young in contemporary societies, which brings with it a beneficial increase in dynamism and creativity, also brings with it a stigmatization of those who are elderly. This stigmatization is not only negative for what it reveals in young, generational selfishness and human indifference but also because it reveals the deformation of the elderly themselves. They often bring forth a necrophiliac thrust characterized by cynicism, apathy, lack

---

restrictive psychopathological sense but in the broader anthropological and cultural sense described, for instance, by Erich Fromm and Axel Honneth. Fromm understands it as the symbolic and cultural unawareness and hidden tendency that aims to diminish, to denigrate, and destroy one's own life and that of others, while Honneth understands it as the process of "reification" and reduction to a thing of everything that is alive. Fromm, *Heart of Man*, 37–61; Honneth, *Verdinglichung*, 11–16.

43. As mentioned before, we will not take this term in its restrictive psychopathological sense but in a broader cultural sense meaning unaware attraction to destructiveness.

44. Ribeyro, *Tentación del fracaso*.

of trust, and resentment against the young based on a narcissism linked to their own past.

Contemporary youth and elderly people, beyond their evident difference and increased separation, share the same reductive view of the future. Young people look at the future mostly as conquest, not as a flourishing event that demands patience and care and that can only be received with gratitude. Elderly people look at it with disappointment because the larger quantity of years earned with scientific, technical, and professional discipline doesn't explain the aborted flourishing characterized by poor quality of physical and relational life. The current opposition between the young generation and the old generation is therefore a false opposition because both categories reinforce, with opposed strategies, a reductive view of life and future, and together defend a masked necrophiliac thrust embodied in the automatic preference of quantity over quality of life. Our young people are already old, even if they appear compulsively active. Our elderly people seem to be young because they are unsatisfied with what they have done, and they still want to live more, not to flourish but to conquer and to achieve even more. Both have a lot of time left, as never before, which they use not to flourish but to accumulate even more quantitative experiences and resources. The inability to flourish, and to flourish in living relationships, has become a cultural involution that mistakenly is sold as historical malice and cultural cunning.

The space–time scheme of other cultures, but also of the generations that preceded us in Western culture, lived in a configuration that privileged old age and flourishing. Old age was seen as the happy completion of a life, a process in which flourishing and the elderly were the embodiment and completion of slow, resilient, inclusive, and complex wisdom that could only develop in the extended arc and in the longtime run of human experience. The space–time scheme of modernity has reversed this formula by privileging not "purpose" (*telos*) but "goal" (*skopos*), not the end but the beginning, not slowness but speed, not complexity but dynamism. In this new cultural scheme, the future is apparently strengthened. In reality, only one type of future is strengthened and not necessarily the best one. The quantitative and linear future of growth and progress, the one that emerges dominant and strengthened, is a future that not only obscures the past but other types of alternative futures as well. The paradox is found in the coincidence and overlapping of victory and defeat of the same future at the same time. Its victory is visible in the radical orientation of trust toward the future, presupposed by all human systems of the present based on efficiency. Its defeat is synchronically expressed in the homogenization of the future that, from multiple differentiated events, becomes a flat and linear future, subservient to growth. That future appears at the same time with overbearing and arrogant contours as it disavows, in principle, any temporal alternative. The vulnerable and slow future of flourishing and old age is then necessarily forgotten and abandoned. In fact, flourishing and old age imply a slow future, less flashy precisely because it is linked to people, to their zigzagging history, to their difficult interaction, to their constant mistakes, hesitations, and doubts, and not to the linear processes of efficiency and production.

The future we have created within our "growth societies" tends to be a necrophiliac future because it is an impersonal future, even if dynamic. It considers and defines itself only with respect to the future as the production of resources and comforts. It does not consider people, or it takes into account only people who have become things and, as such, are functional to efficiency.[45] Ours is not a culture oriented toward the future of people but only toward the future as a calculation. In fact, the future linked to people cannot be calculated because it is imbued with that incommensurability typical of living things. It is, consequently, no longer part of the social equation that interests us. Calculation, on the other hand, presupposes measurability, of processes and, therefore, also of people who have become things. The future, understood as the flourishing and fullness of the elderly, is completely unknown to us. A living future and a life-promoting future always depends on people, not on processes. In fact, we have elderly people, and in ever greater numbers, who are without a future precisely because the future they offer us is dark: a future full of regrets, ironies, pessimism, tiredness, and lack of faith in younger generations. It is a compulsive future of adults who are not satisfied with what they have in the present and try to reach what they believe they have missed in the past. Paradoxically, the future preached by Adventism has taken much of that same necrophiliac drift.

Adventism, in fact, tends to think about the future only as a religious and prophetic process, not in terms of people and relationships between people, thus contradicting its own name. The Latins had two words to designate the future: "futurum" and "adventus."[46] "Futurum" designated the future linked to temporal processes and mechanisms of various kinds

---

45. Esposito, *Persone e le cose*, 3–35.
46. See Gutierrez Salazar, *Beyond the Bible*, 499–511.

inferred from the present. "Adventus" described the future linked to the unpredictability and incommensurability of people. The future as "futurum" can be calculated starting from data in the present. The future as "adventus" can't be calculated but only waited for, as we wait for somebody not knowing when that person will arrive. By thinking of the future as a prophetic process and doctrinal precision rather than as the future of people, Adventism tends to deform itself and lose its soul. It's not enough to think of Christ's second coming with the "adventus" category, in order to save his incommensurability, if we reserve to all other human players the category of "futurum," with its reductive measurability. If people, who are God's incarnation (see Matt 25), are taken away their incommensurability through precise and rigorous doctrines and prophecies, then God becomes a predictable God, without incommensurability. When that happens, Adventism has becomes a precise but cold futurism.

The future preached by Adventism is too often thought of as a cold process of prophetic precision and doctrinal orthodoxy, which, to remain objective, must avoid being contaminated by the hesitation and irregularity typical of experiences connected to people. In order to save Adventism, then, Adventists are ready to sacrifice people; but by sacrificing them, "Adventism" becomes just a kind of "futurism" based on reliable and honorable religious or biblical processes but detached from people. People, not only Adventists but non-Adventist people of other secular and religious communities who will never become Adventists, are those who truly constitute us as true Adventists because they challenge, provoke, and promote in us what really matters: respect, recognition, love, and care. While "futurum" is about counting and classifying people, "adventus" is about waiting, loving, and admiring them. That's precisely what Adventism seems to have lost. We don't transmit life; we don't get life from others. For Adventists, people have become things we need to classify. As such, we don't love them as much as we are not loved by them. But by doing so we become a lifeless and inert community. Most non-Adventist people don't love us; they only respect us for what we do, for the discipline and commitment we show. We conclude by saying that they don't love us because they don't love the truth. By so doing, we incur into two vulgar mistakes: first, by underestimating them as God's incarnation, and second, by idolizing Adventism as the full and last incarnation of God. When a critique of Adventism automatically becomes a critique of God himself, we have gone beyond what is theologically permissible and appropriate. We have an upside-down world.

Real future "adventus" is only relatively concerned with truth. Essentially, it is concerned with life. And this theological equation is applicable also to God. More than true, God is life. His truth makes alive all with which he comes into contact. It seems that Adventism has chosen the opposite alternative, that of "reifying" (reducing to things) all that we touch, all that is, and aspire to be alive. All our missiology, eschatology, and catechism seem to be too much impregnated by this "reifying" attitude and aspiration. And this obsession with classifying instead of resurrecting people through love and care is the greatest necrophiliac temptation we must resist if we want to preserve and promote a living Adventism. It's not Adventism that will save people but rather people who will save Adventism. This distancing from people occurs in Adventism through a double modality.

The first is an endogenous modality. Adventism does not trust its young people. It believes in them only if they maintain what the pioneers have created. It is a subtle and refined way not only to keep its young people caged but also a sneaky strategy to not believe in them. The history of the present is read in light of the primordial history of the pioneers and is therefore condemned to be a repetition of what has already happened. The second modality is exogenous. Adventism does not believe in others, neither as individuals nor, even less, as groups, or believes in them only when they agree with Adventism. For Adventism, others are only a reason for deviance and contamination. We do not see in them a positive reason and motivation for updating and reformulating what we believe. Adventism does not like to reformulate itself; it only likes to repeat itself. It repeats itself precisely because it tends to erase the new interlocutors who are the engine and the irreplaceable instances that trigger reformulations. Indeed, Adventism only likes listeners, not interlocutors—those who, by nature, ask new questions and are unsatisfied with the usual answers.

Flourishing as much as future (Advent) are both tightly linked to people. Without people, flourishing becomes production and future becomes calculation. Without people, Adventism marks its own involution and its own rigidity. Hence, the aversion and stigmatization of ecumenism that Adventism takes as a compact block from which to keep others away, or sometimes, to recognize partially, only because of a relative and centripetal benefit for Adventism. By relativizing ecumenism, Adventism relativizes and weakens itself. But Adventism does not want to hear about these complex processes that demand patience and trust. It only likes the visible and satisfying clarity of immediate certainties.

Part II: Vulnerability and Flourishing

For this reason, Adventism is not an alternative to the necrophiliac tendency of our time and its linear, but closed, future but rather a perfect expression of it, even if, on secondary and peripheral dimensions, it pretends to fight tooth and nail. Adventism, like the contemporary culture that surrounds it, are both future-phobic precisely because they are people-phobic. They are afraid of the future because they are afraid of the otherness embodied in people—an otherness that escapes all planning and prophetic meticulous and rigorous descriptions. Consequently, out of necessity and sublimation, both continue to talk about the future and people, but at the core, they mean only processes and mechanisms. By speaking about the future and people in this way, they do not convey joy or hope but only anguish, both in the form of distrust about the future of others and in the form of obsession with their own future. Contemporary culture and the Adventism that prolongs it, even when it contradicts it, are therefore anxiogenic by nature, precisely because they have stopped loving and letting themselves be surprised by people and by their incommensurability.

It is not for nothing that the future of the West easily becomes necrophiliac. As philosopher Umberto Galimberti reminds us in his book *The Decline of the West*, its basis presupposes the decline as a structural perspective and final destiny.[47] Rapid realization and sudden decline, dynamism and tiredness, efficiency and apathy, euphoria and depression, are closely linked and interdependent in the cultural western profile. "The era of emptiness" is one way to characterize our historical period, according to Gilles Lipovetsky.[48] It is sequential and dependent on our radical and compulsive dynamism. There is a maniacal soul hidden in the performative West that forces it to tiredness and dejection, writes psychoanalyst Christopher Bollas.[49] The West lives on a cultural and social level of "bipolar" dysfunction (manic-depressive) that it wants to limit only individual pathology. In fact, sociologist Alain Ehrenberg notes that Western culture experiences a kind of cultural bipolar dysfunction composed by two related moments: a manic and compulsive moment that he describes as "the worship of performance,"[50] and by a depressive moment, in which exhaustion is inevitable, that he describes as "the weariness of the self,"[51] which is the soul

---

47. Galimberti, *Tramonto dell'Occidente*, 23–54.
48. Lipovetsky, *Ère du vide*, 9–24.
49. Bollas, *Meaning and Melancholia*, 7–13.
50. Ehrenberg, *Worship of Performance*, 12–25.
51. Ehrenberg, *Weariness of the Self*, 6–22.

mate of efficient individuals. What happens on an individual level is then reproduced on a social level. Both influence themselves reciprocally. Beyond individual experience, depression is a cultural condition facilitated by the radical efficiency and discipline Western culture has always promoted and praised. The emphasis on speed and immediate productivity (sunrise) triggers, almost automatically, tiredness, decay, and decline (sunset), wrote Oswald Spengler a century ago in his famous text *The Decline of the West*.[52] He compared eight civilizations of world history. He wrote in particular about the ancient Greek civilization characterized as "Apollonian" for the symmetry, the sense of limit, and containment that it tended to create. In contrast, he cited the "Faustian" radical dynamism and obsessive discipline typical of the West, with the sequential tiredness and decline that it spontaneously draws.

Necrophilia does not always presuppose failed, deviant, and transgressive individuals but the contrary people who have succeeded. Ethically and technically reliable people who have, in one way or another, lived experiences of flourishing are perfect candidates to embody necrophiliac impulses. In one of our previous texts, we have called this necrophiliac drive, transversal and structural to the contemporary world, "cultural positivism."[53] That which is hidden and sublimated by the efficiency that current sociocultural systems guarantee to perfection, but which, at the same time, behave as hiding and dissimulating symptoms of this necrophiliac drive.

Necrophilia is, in fact, a priority theme imposed on us by a serious reflection on Ps 1 (the second stanza, verses 4–6), but also by a careful cultural analysis of the time in which we live. Necrophilia is not only that evident evil that we all reject through an instinctive sense of self-preservation but also that subtle evil that bewitches us, seduces us, and draws us toward itself with our own consent. It is a kind of unfortunate destiny that enchants and grips us, toward which we seem almost forced to go. Not the risk of good, which often appears monotonous and obvious, but the risk of evil that, instead, seems to offer us immeasurable novelty and intensity. The flourishing described in the first stanza (verses 1–3) thus seem weaker than the alienation and human destructiveness that imposes itself on us with the force of unbeatable determination, described in the second stanza (verses 4–6). Indeed, this negative force, originally outside us, is greater than us, gives birth within us,

---

52. Spengler, *Decline of the West*, 12–34.
53. See Gutierrez Salazar, *Beyond the Bible*, 418–26.

and, with our complicity, to an internal drive toward self-destruction and death. It is, paradoxically, as Peruvian writer Julio Ramon Ribeyro says, a real "temptation"[54]—the temptation of death, of self-destructiveness, the "temptation to fail." Freud described it as a drive that pushes us toward death ("Todestriebe"/*Tanatos*), opposed to the parallel drive of life ("Lebenstriebe"/*Eros*).[55] Both drives live in each of us without our knowledge and condition what we do and what we are beyond our own awareness.

It is not easy to understand what is naturally healthy, and what is artificial and appears healthy but is not. Even more difficult to understand is where destruction hides and what forms it takes, which often emerges more as "auto-destruction" than "allo-destruction."[56] Finally, and consequently, it has become equally difficult to distinguish "affirmation" from "negation" of life. Contemporary human and cultural phenomena have become tremendously ambivalent. What seems to affirm life often ends up denying it. In other historical periods, the profile of situations and protagonists was clearer and more linear. Today, it is not.

In fact, the experience of flourishing, introduced in Ps 1 as an experience to be desired and sought, is itself imbued with a marked ambivalence. Qualitative "development" (flourishing) is easily confused with quantitative "growth" (performative efficiency). In economics, "growth" and "development" both describe a process of improvement. But they do not mean the same thing at all. "Growth" expresses a quantitative improvement, important but insufficient to account for a qualitative improvement. "Development" expresses a qualitatively different improvement that must be considered in order to truly speak an economic or spiritual process worthy of the name.

In economics, for instance, the surprising and miraculous "growth" of BRICS countries (Brazil, Russia, India, China, South Africa, etc.), is unfortunately inversely proportional with their "development." The criteria for "development" are different than those that determine "growth." In economics, a main criterium for "growth" is the measure of the annual Gross Domestic Profit (GDP). Criteria for "development" are instead the reliability of institutions, the division of powers, respect of minorities, etc. Criteria for "spiritual growth" are baptisms, institutional programming, financial resources, or facilities. Criteria for "spiritual development" are instead the

---

54. Ribeyro, *Temptation of Failing*.
55. Freud, *Beyond the Pleasure Principle*, 2–23.
56. "Allo-destruction" means "destruction of others."

guarantee of internal alternatives, respect of various level of governance, quality of satisfaction, recognition of other churches' mission and ministries, etc.

Many positive experiences that we have in various areas of our life, including religion, that we think contribute to our "development" only contribute to our "growth," thus triggering a mechanism that Axel Honneth calls "reification of life,"[57] which is a subtle and refined form of this necrophiliac drive typical of our time. The necrophiliac drive is not only present in those who do not believe, as believers would think, but in believers themselves when they do not know how to distinguish between spiritual "growth" and "development."

a. Necrophiliac Aggregates

Necrophilia numbs and paralyzes life, not always directly but also indirectly, through a net of mechanisms that, by hiding it, potentiate it. For this reason, a necrophiliac thrust is not immediately visible. Its unmasking and deciphering are sometimes slow and demanding. In fact, present cultural necrophilia is composed of two anomalies. It is the perfect superposition of a "deficit" and an "excess."[58] It is a mixture of a deficit of "enchantment" and an excess of "efficiency." This "excess" of efficiency, in its various possible forms, is given by the cult of precision. Numbers have replaced figures; measurement has swallowed complexity. Similarly, the "deficit" is the result of the now chronic inability to think and experience the symbols in its structural ambivalence and paradox. The failure of the simulacra of symbols that abound in today's marketplace of meaning, precisely as an intent to recapture a symbol that eludes us, does not depend on their nature, per se, but on the context and system that behaves as a shredder of meaning. The eventual existential and spiritual respite that some symbols and myths try to create in us is not functional for a change of perspective, a necessary cultural metanoia. It serves only as a moment of pause for an even more radical functioning of our pragmatic system, devoid of true symbols and metaphors. It swallows up and paralyzes any intent for new meaning.

57. Honneth, *Verdinglichung*, 11–16.

58. This dual component will be called differently according to the perspective chosen by various authors. Massimo Cacciari speaks, for example, of "Paradise and Shipwreck" as characterizing the contemporary man already described by Musil. Cacciari, *Paradiso e naufragio*, 10–22.

Part II: Vulnerability and Flourishing

It is what Spanish philosopher Eugenio Trías calls "the disease of the West,"[59] a careful analysis of modernity and postmodernity, rightly and fairly recognizes the uniqueness of modern thought. Although it is unparalleled in its dynamism, he ends up categorizing it as structurally reductive thought. According to Trías, the limitation of this thought lies in its inability to mythicize. It sublimates this by presenting itself only as enlightened thought (Enlightenment). The symbolic and mythical defect is sold by modern and postmodern thought as a virtue. Its inability to mythicize, which this chronic defect evidences, is a true form of cultural involution that Trías describes as the structural and unconscious disease of the West. The West is wise and well-informed. Yet, it is unaware of its own discomfort and cognitive compulsion that it tries to sell as science to others.

The unconscious mechanism of its articulation aggregates the problem. This superimposition of "deficit" and "excess" is its typical mode of dissimulation. Because it would be too humiliating to acknowledge that one has "killed the meaning" of God, nature, humanity, groups, and texts, one unconsciously proceeds to hide that defect behind an extraordinary "achievement," behind a cognitive virtue. One claims to know more when, in fact, one knows less. This mechanism of unconscious concealment occurs through what Freud called "reactive formation."[60] It is a defense mechanism of the self, of one's identity, of one's cultural pride, through a strategy of concealment.

In this secondary defense mechanism, an unmentionable thought is sublimated through the creation of a virtuous thought. A marked unmentionable sexual weakness, for example, is hidden unknowingly behind extreme purism and moral rigor. Similarly, the unmentionable chronic inability to create living, transformative meaning is covered up by scintillating analytical dexterity and quick, reactive thinking. It is what Christopher Bollas calls, in a more radical and provocative way, the "manic," inordinately alert, restless, and compulsive component of the Western soul and thinking.[61] One is compelled to know more because one knows less and poorly.

59. Trías, *Pensar la religión*, 99–111.
60. McWilliams, *Psychoanalytic Diagnosis*, 140–42.
61. Christopher Bollas makes, as a psychoanalyst, a psychological analysis of the cultural dysfunctions of the West, not by improperly extending individual clinical diagnoses to more general cultural situations but by censoring parallels—similarities in the mechanisms that highlight the psychological component of the political, economic, and cultural problems of the present, which is usually overlooked. Bollas, *Meaning and Melancholia*, 7–13.

Why should we underline this cultural positivism and the necrophiliac thrust it brings? Because it results in an apathy and symbolic illiteracy that forces Western humanity to propose "empty forms" as resolutions erected as a universal parameter. It's like wanting to sell ice to Eskimos or *papas* (potatoes) to Peruvians. The West, through sophisticated informational, educational, and advertising strategies, wants to teach people of the South how to group, how to manage nature, how to believe in God, how to read texts, and what symbols to know. This is cultural nihilism. It is emptiness presented as fullness, form as substance, quantity as quality, growth as development, complication as complexity, contract as a gift, or sense as meaning.

Love for efficiency and success easily becomes a sophisticated form of necrophilia typical of our time. Necrophiliac impulses can be found in dysfunctional as much as in virtuous people. If necrophilia is the love of things over persons, even the love of good ideas or good doctrines can convey and manifest necrophiliac attitudes over time. Necrophilia doesn't include uniquely repulsive material things as corpses, garbage, or debris but also beautiful things, such as nice houses, cars, computers, or musical instruments, which are inanimate. And the problem doesn't exist in lifeless things as such. We need them and they are part of life. The problem is to attribute them a priority over living things. Until proven otherwise, not only material things but also practices, ideas, doctrines, systems, books (including the Bible) are inert in the sense that they don't have movement and direction on their own. When we prefer them to people, they function as reified fetishes that distance us from life. Loving sofas is not a problem. But there is a problem when we love them more than we love the children who dirty them. Culturally and anthropologically, there is more value in children who defile sofas than in clean and fragrant sofas themselves. The same can be said about sacred things, such as rituals, programs, books, or doctrines. There is more value in people who transgress them than in pure, pristine, and spotless rituals for the simple reason that "sacred things" are more things than sacred. The only real sacred thing is life, even when that life is compromised, halved, threatened, and withered.

In Ps 1, second stanza, the wicked are described as necrophiliac because they seek life in the wrong things. But the first stanza attributes latent necrophilia also to pious believers if they stop loving the right things. Right things are means, not goals in themselves. Right things must always be superseded and overcome by life and by promotion of life. The wicked, tied to unjust and biased things, and the pious, tied to just and unbiased things, both express the same necrophilia that is only different in degree and proportions. It is not the law and the right things we do in obedience to it that make our experience a living experience. We can call ourselves blessed only if we are like the tree, whose life presupposes obedience to the laws of nature, which, in addition, covers itself with beauty and gifts. A living believer is not characterized by obedience to the law, a type of refined necrophilia, but the additional flourishing of that obedience. In a certain sense, the entire psalm speaks of necrophilia: the first stanza (verses 1–3) of a refined necrophilia, that of the legalist, and the second stanza (verses 4–6), the visible and bold necrophilia of the transgressor.

Let's come back to Charles Taylor's description of necrophilia that he understands as an aggregate of various attitudes. He calls this necrophilia a "malaise," intending by this a kind of "mild necrophilia," which is nonetheless perverse. On the contrary, "mild necrophilia" is more dangerous because it's more transversal, unaware, and chronic. Taylor particularly is interested in describing three contemporary phenomena that are linked to three positive events of our recent history that, over time, deform themselves and nourish this necrophiliac trend of modern societies: the dynamism introduced by the individual; the force of our programming reason; and the mobilizing power of democracy. His analysis particularly considers the side effects of these virtues that lead him to question the form that modern development has taken. Taylor pauses in his discussion of the chronic anomalies of modernity and its dysfunctions to particularly describe three of them that he calls the "Malaise of Modernity":[62] self-referential individualism, instrumental reason, and mild despotism. Taylor writes the following:

> These, then, are the three malaises about modernity that I want to deal with in this book. The first fear is about what we might call a loss of meaning, the fading of moral horizons. The second concerns the eclipse of ends in the face of rampant instrumental reason. And the third is about the loss of freedom."[63]

Taylor is not alone in considering the simultaneity of different phenomena and trying to decipher their implicit convergence. Different cultural phenomena may share the same temporal and spatial setting. They may also trigger interactions that duplicate their effect. These would remain underdiagnosed if they were described in isolation. The synergy between

---

62. Taylor, *Malaise of Modernity*, 1–12.
63. Taylor, *Malaise of Modernity*, 10.

contemporary phenomena, more often than not, is implicit and hidden. A special effort of attention, not without risk, must be made in order to bring out the mutual enhancement of their effects.

Taylor considers the disenchanting effect and the anomalies of these three cultural phenomena on human life and experience.[64] Individualism, instrumental reason, and mild despotism have as their common effect the mechanization of human life and its reduction to a programmable and predictable reality. This creates dynamism and efficiency in the system, which, though short-lived, life is depowered in the long run. Life is reduced to its functionality and the results it produces. Taylor describes our culture as a typical form of cultural positivism whose main characteristic is the disenchantment of life and reality.

Disenchantment and atomism are narrowly related. Disenchantment arises from an atomization of reality, of which social individualism is only one manifestation. Atomism breaks down, disintegrates, separates, and isolates in order to achieve more. This cultural anomaly atomizes reality and creates an apparent enchantment that is embodied in the efficiency and productivity of the system. This is why the disenchantment described by Taylor is actually a powerful but short-lived enchantment. It is an artificially inflated enchantment that, immediately after its powerful initial effect, produces only dispersion, detachment, isolation, and emptiness. Similarly, the interaction of these three cultural dysfunctionalities (atomism, globalization, and regulation) creates a powerful but short-lived effect of success and gain. Immediately afterward, it leaves apathy, emptiness, and self-destruction. A compulsion to start over again sets in, creating a clear cultural mechanism of dependence that pushes us to desperately search for even more efficiency. We try to correct the distortions of too much efficiency with updated forms of the same efficiency.

The ultimate effect of this dysfunctional aggregate is the death of a culture. This seems to be a strong and seemingly excessive statement. In fact, though, the disenchantment of the world produced by the radicalization of these three phenomena triggers a clear movement of sense-weariness that may well be described as a necrophiliac drive.[65] It is not that all contemporary culture is necrophiliac. In some ways, it is vibrant and dynamic; but it conveys a destructive drive that tends to cage life.

---

64. Taylor, *Secular Age*, 539.

65. This is the term used explicitly by Erich Fromm to characterize the direction of contemporary culture. Fromm, *Heart of Man*, 37–61.

It tries to order life, to neutralize it. To the "death of God,"[66] as a symbol of transcendence, embodied in the typically modern motto *etsi deus non daretur* (as if God did not exist), we have added *etsi homo non daretur* (the death of our neighbor).[67] As Luigi Zoja suggests, we have become chronically indifferent to others, creating an individualistic lifestyle that may well be framed in the parallel motto as descriptive of this second narrowing of meaning and life. As if this were not enough, things have also become dead objects.[68] We have stopped experiencing the real.[69] It is possible to add a third parallel motto that describes the necrophiliac tendency of contemporary societies this way: *etsi mundus non daretur* (as if the world did not exist). In such a necrophiliac context, meaning and the meaning of life can neither survive nor be reborn.

This necrophiliac tendency is manifested today in the strong push to dematerialize things and the world. Things tend to lose consistency and become ethereal. This does not happen through the intervention of an external authoritarian force that prohibits us from enjoying things. Neither is it caused by an extreme idealism that, as in the past, privileged the intelligible world at the expense of the tangible world without denying it. Today, the evanescence of things occurs through an immanent phenomenon produced by us, namely, the explosion of information. The power of information causes things to lose value and consistency. Information about things is now worth more than the things themselves. Digitization is dematerializing our world and our relationship with it. This is evidenced by the loss, for example, of memories, because memories are always memories of concrete things. Memory has been replaced by data. We live in the age of the realm of data. Data is the prevalence of the information of things over things themselves.

This loss of things automatically drags with it a loss of the world, of its order and consistency. For the world is made, as Hannah Arendt recalled, by things that give it stability.[70] Only things that stabilize life give consistency to the world. Today, we tend to live more on "Google Earth" and the "Cloud" than on the real world. Information tends to cover things and

---

66. According to the famous aphorism coined by Nietzsche. Nietzsche, *Gaia scienza*; Vahanian, *Death of God*.

67. Zoja, *Morte del prossimo*, 12–31.

68. Bodei, *Vita delle cose*.

69. Han, *Non cose*, 21–35.

70. Arendt, *Vita active*, 7–17.

prevail over them. It is to this intangible relationship with reality that a new kind of relationship with truth also belongs. Truth has always been a factual truth, a truth expressed and conquered in the world of things. The digital world puts an end to this kind of truth and gives rise to a post-factual truth. The information age is the age of a post-factual truth, of which fake news is merely an extension and manifestation. Today's truth is a volatile truth, located and articulated above facts and independent of them. That is why the concreteness of things does not count as corroboration of the truth claim, exposed or defended. The only thing that counts is the immediate and explosive effect of a truth without things. The effect and efficiency of truth has taken over, not its connection with reality.

This realm of information that dispenses with things dispenses with the space of things as well. Things rooted in space that slow down our relationship with them also employ a particular kind of temporality. It is a fast and hurried temporality. The temporality of the new media and information is an accelerated temporality.

The realm of information deforms our relationship with space and time. It creates a space that is fast because it is aseptic of presences and things. Time that is fast is also aseptic and neutral because it is devoid of presences that contaminate it by slowing it down. The dematerialized world of information works with a caricature of space and time. Informational space and time are fast and performant because they are completely dissociated from things, the world, and life.

The world of living things requires a slow and contaminated space and time. This is what Marc Augé, regarding space, calls "place," as opposed to a fast and aseptic space that he calls "non-place."[71] At the same time, Marramao speaks of *kairos*,[72] as opposed to an accelerated time, which he defines, taking a phrase from Shakespeare's *Hamlet*,[73] as "off-axis time," or "dromomania," or "hurry syndrome."[74]

The slow time and contaminated space of the world of things stabilize life and give it a framework that is the world of things. A different ethics is articulated that values loyalty, commitment, promise, observances, obligations, and resilience. In the world of information, all this tends to disappear,

---

71. Augé, *Non-luoghi*, 20–31.
72. Marramao, *Kairos*, 9–21.
73. "The time is out of joint" in Hamlet's mouth. Marramao, *Passione del presente*, 101.
74. Marramao, *Passione del presente*, 94.

to be replaced by a validation of efficiency, results, immediacy, speed, force of impact, and strength of numbers. The world of information accelerates meaning and changes habits and attitudes. One takes note of the world's data without being able to know the world. One travels everywhere without experiencing the places one visits. One increases communication processes without being part of a community. One stores data without creating memories. One exponentially increases the number of friends without really discovering each other.

Passion and libidinal energies are also no longer oriented to things but to non-things, to information. Fetishism is reversed because it no longer fetishes things but data. Data are just a concentrate of information. Things and events are reduced to measurement. The infosphere,[75] a new reference reality, is the world of non-things—the world of data. These transparent data survive in functional and circumstantial connections. They do not create stories. Only narratives assemble and sew events into plots—into real stories. The digital, because it lives on the fragments of the world (data are fragments), does not create any story and it does not create memory. It gives birth to what Vilém Flusser calls the parallel world of the worship of images, i.e., "idolatry," and the worship of text as a collection of data, i.e., "textolatry."[76] The world of things has ceased to exist, and we have entered the world of "non-things."[77]

In such a necrophiliac context, the meaning of life and texts cannot survive, much less be born again. There is an urgent need for *Auferstehung*,[78] a cultural resurrection that will enable the flourishing of life and meaning against all necrophiliac threats and insinuations.

b. Resisting Necrophilia: "The Resurrection of the Other"

The only way to resist necrophilia is to flourish. Even defending life is not enough because many mechanisms articulated to defend life, which effectively protect and, to some degree, even promote life, express sophisticated and mild forms of necrophilia. Building a home, working for food, struggling to get instruction, reading the Bible, attending church, distributing

75. Floridi, *Pensare l'infosfera*, 12–23.
76. Flusser, *Cultura dei media*, 23–35.
77. Han, *Non cose*, 6–19.
78. "Resurrection" in German; for the additional and specific reference, we will make to Gustav Mahler.

religious literature, even praying can give us a sense of living but are not necessarily expressions of healthy flourishing. Working for our own flourishing can express a kind of artificial living and, in a paradoxical and narcissistic way, affirm our necrophilia.

Flourishing, essentially, has to do with caring and promoting life, not our own live or the live of our tribe, but the life of all living beings. In this sense, true flourishing happens only when we work for other people's flourishing, when we defend others, when we contribute to rescue, protect, and affirm the lives of our neighbors, human and nonhuman.

Only when our neighbors are alive can we be certain of being alive ourselves. For this reason, the necessary cultural and symbolical resurrection is not our own resurrection but the resurrection of the other. As Mungi Ngomane reminds us, it's not "my" but "our lives" that really matter.[79] In fact, her Ubuntu background pushes her to condense Ubuntu philosophy in the sentences: "I am because you are," or, "I exist when somebody starts looking at me."

Flourishing is that resonance for life that supports my own resonance. Hartmut Rosa says the best way to overcome necrophiliac temptations, of which alienation from others is the main sign, is resonance. Resonance is a way of life in which people feel touched, involved, and challenged by other people, places, and objects that previously produced no echo in us. From an existential point of view, we all know what it means to be touched by someone's gaze or voice, a piece of music we listen to, a book we read, or a place we visit. The ability to feel affected by something and, in turn, develop an intrinsic interest in the part of the world that affects us, is a central element of any positive way of relating to the world. In contrast to alienation, which stops the flow of life, resonance reconnects this flow. It is defined by two essential movements.

The first movement is that of "af-fection." Affection is not the ability to feel something but rather the ability to welcome, to be touched (affected) by what comes to us from outside. From being numb to the voices of others, from the muteness of things and people that we have turned into manipulatable and dumb objects, we become instead, perhaps for the first time, capable of being touched by voices that we stop manipulating. Affection is the afferent pathway that reaches us from the outside, creating a feeling that is not our own but simply the effect of others coming to us. The world is no longer indifferent but speaks to us.

---

79. Ngomane, *Everyday Ubuntu*, 11–15.

Part II: Vulnerability and Flourishing

The second movement is that of "e-motion." This is not the ability to feel something closed in ourselves but rather the momentum that starts from us toward others after we have been resurrected by their voice. E-emotion is the centrifugal movement that allows us for the first time, because we are alive, to offer something meaningful and living from ourselves to others. Emotion is the efferent way from us to others. We are no longer indifferent to the world, but we are able to give something alive, our voice, our meaning to this external world.

Flourishing is resurrection, and resurrection is the resurrection of others. This is the message of Gustav Mahler's second symphony, which has precisely the title, *Auferstehung* (resurrection).[80]

Overthrowing a positivist culture that encloses life and meaning in the mechanism of a rational calculation and equation is possible only by a culture of life, by a change of language,[81] by a spiritual resurrection. This is why the Spirit of life must again become the center of a spiritual and cultural revival. This is not the spirit of sanctification, the spirit of the Bible, or even less, the spirit of a particular confession. The Spirit of life is the inclusive and universal Spirit whose horizon of action is not the narrow horizon of one denomination, one culture, one historical period, one territory, one party, one affiliation. It is the horizon that includes every form of life, human and nonhuman. The renewal of our culture, the recovery of the meaning of life and of biblical meaning, and, in a broader perspective, the recovery of meaning in an ecological sense, comes through the "pneumatological turn."

Why use such a strong metaphor as *Auferstehung*, moving it from its natural biblical–theological context and applying it to all of culture? For several reasons, but the one Martha Nussbaum suggests is especially important.[82] Commenting on Mahler's second symphony, she describes the real change as

---

80. On the meaning of *Auferstehung* in Mahler, there will be various interpretations. Martha Nussbaum will favor that of passage or rupture. Norman Lebrecht stands in the same wake as Nussbaum but thinks that Mahler's symphonies, and the second one, represent a cultural turning point that changed the way we think about the world. Lebrecht, *Why Mahler*, 72–80.

81. This is what Greffré suggests when he writes, "In any case, it must be known that there is no creation of a new language of faith without it leading to a reinterpretation of the Christian message." Geffré, *Credere e interpretare*, 56.

82. In her book on the intelligence of the emotions, Nussbaum actually discusses Mahler at various, even quantitatively important, moments, but it is in the fourteenth chapter, devoted entirely to Mahler, that she analyzes and comments on Mahler's second symphony, *Auferstehung*. See Nussbaum, *Intelligenza delle emozioni*, 721–43.

one that must come from outside. After all, *Auferstehung*, unlike the immortality of the soul,[83] is a typical relational experience with the Totally Other. One is not resurrected, or one is not born based on one's own power, through an exercise of one's own will and awareness. This happens solely through reliance on the intervention of an Other who comes to us from outside.

The rediscovery of meaning in the West cannot take place, according to Nussbaum, through refinement or innovation within the same modern system. This would lead to the perpetuation of the anomaly that it tries to correct. The system must be "broken" from the outside through alternative forms of thinking that cause real telluric movements, epistemological shocks, earthquakes of thought. These other thoughts have as their common denominator the motivational, perspective, and symbolic force of emotions. The renewal of meaning can only take place through an *Auferstehung*, a resurrection of symbolic forms of thought, which have been forgotten and stigmatized by the West in past centuries.

This is the urgent and recurring call of Bernhard Waldenfels in his *Phenomenology of the Other*.[84] The central feature of this discovery of the other, according to Waldenfels, is not the relevance of our question. Because our word is never primary, it is the vulnerability of our response. It is not initially configured as a question but as a response to a voice that is there before us, that precedes us and interrogates us.[85] When the other resumes its place, we regain our vulnerability, the foundation of a possible relationality. Relationality is never the certainty of the self over the other. It is the reliance on the other of a vulnerable self. Such vulnerability does not make life precarious. It makes it full through the non-manipulation of the other, who always remains a "stranger," not a threat, but a simultaneous source of "extraordinariness." The other as "strange," "foreign," and "extraordinary" determines the cornerstones of an anthropology of vulnerability.[86]

---

83. Jürgen Moltmann reads the main difference between "immortality of the soul" and "resurrection" through the category of relationality, which, in the former, is missing while in the latter, it is the heart of it. Moltmann, *Avvento di Dio*, 71–92.

84. Conventionally, this title is translated to English as *Phenomenology of the Alien* but, in my opinion, "Other" is a better translation. Waldenfels's entire *oeuvre* is traversed by this central motif of the Other. See the four volumes of his *Phenomenology of the Other*: Waldenfels, *Studien zur Phänomenologie des Fremdes*, vols. 1–4. See especially Waldenfels, *Topographie des Fremdes*, 16–53.

85. Waldenfels, *Grundmotive einer Phänomenologie*, 56–67.

86. Waldenfels, *Estraneo, straniero, straordinario*, 13–36.

How can we hold it all together: the resurrection of the Other, untampered sense, *kenosis*, vulnerability, immanent life? Through the Spirit. Pneumatology makes possible the recomposing of meaning through the rediscovery of the others who impose themselves on us through their *Auferstehung*. This is the most important passage in the Mahlerian interpretation of *Auferstehung*, as commented on by Nussbaum in relation to Mahler's second symphony. Life as flourishing is possible only through the resurrection of the other through the Spirit.

c. The Need for a New Language

To say all this, the flourishing life, the resurrection of the Other, the supporting role of the Spirit in promoting life, we need a new language. The change of language does not add a complement of meaning. It changes the sense and grounds it differently. It is what C. Geffré calls the "ilemorphic" property of language. It consists of a change of sense by changing the form of language. Geffré writes,

> Language is the very locus of meaning, and when you change language, you change meaning. It is what I call an "ilemorphic" conception of language: just as it is not given to dissociate the soul from the body, so one cannot dissociate the soul of language from its vehicle, its textual body.[87]

The renewal of culture and religion and the construction of new meanings, made possible by a different look at life, starts from a rediscovery of pneumatology. The "pneumatological turn" urges us to have a change of language suited to catch what is new. It simultaneously urges us to revisit and reinterpret the whole Christian message.[88] In this regard, writes Claude Geffré,

> So the search for a new language, for a reformulation of dogma is not simply "adaptation" to the most common understanding of the faithful, it is a risky operation, it is an operation that leads to a reinterpretation of dogma.[89]

---

87. Geffré, *Credere e interpretare*, 57. Geffré makes his own the typical "hilemorphic" Aristotelian conception that, unlike Plato, who spoke of a sense (idea) independently of its container (body), every idea is linked to its form. Moreover, this close relationship between ideas and forms is also supported by P. Ricœur when he speaks of the indissolubility between "kerygmatic content" and "literary form." Ricœur, *Ermeneutica filosofica*, 80–85.

88. Di Ceglie, *God, the Good*, 56–76.

89. Geffré, *Credere e interpretare*, 56.

The English title of Nussbaum's book *Upheavals of Thought* conveys this sense of rupture,[90] which is only presupposed and hidden in the Italian title, *L'intelligenza delle emozioni*.[91] Nussbaum describes five forms of thought that break the ordered but predictable linearity of the West's cultural positivism: first, an ethics of prerational choices;[92] second, the empathically fast and immediate thinking of animals;[93] third, the slow and metaphorical thinking of non-Western peoples;[94] fourth, the non-sequential and instinctively trusting thinking of children;[95] and fifth, the immaterial thinking and universally inclusive aesthetics of music.[96] In describing this fifth way, the musical way, Nussbaum comments on Mahler and his symphonic work. She presents it as an eventual prototype of a new kind of language that is capable of unhinging and overthrowing the cultural positivism we have so far tried to describe.

What do these alternative thoughts and languages provoke? It is not the empowerment of the one who knows. It is not the greater precision and exhaustiveness of the cognitive processes in play. It is not the malleability and measurability of entities reduced to clear and distinct objects; it is rather their resistance and their unavailability. Is the *Auferstehung* (resurrection) of the others' otherness perceived and preserved by the intelligence of emotions? Through emotions, we enter in communion with the realities we know not by controlling them but by loving them in their unavailability. We are not masters but companions, not observers but lovers, not helpers but helpless, in a relational process of empathy and communion. These alternative strategies of knowing and saying are typical and classical strategies of "recognition" of the other,[97] which the West has misplaced and prematurely and cynically called "superstition."

The *Auferstehung* of the other, as a condition of social resonance, necessarily requires and demands the introduction of a new language. Others cannot be discovered with our current language. They can't be thought of in

---

90. Literally in English, "earthquakes of thought."
91. Nussbaum, *Intelligenza delle emozioni*.
92. Nussbaum, *Intelligenza delle emozioni*, 37–116.
93. Nussbaum, *Intelligenza delle emozioni*, 117–75.
94. Nussbaum, *Intelligenza delle emozioni*, 177–218.
95. Nussbaum, *Intelligenza delle emozioni*, 219–92.
96. Nussbaum, *Intelligenza delle emozioni*, 305–56.
97. This entire section, the first section of the book, is articulated on the pivotal category of "Recognition." See Nussbaum, *Intelligenza delle emozioni*, 35.

its specificities with the same linguistic categories that have for a long time denied them. Our common language is a functional and positivist language that considers only communalities, the average and standard elements of people and events. It does not, as such, envisage the existence of the other. It anonymizes it, objectifies it, neutralizes it. Mahler's music instead, in Nussbaum's interpretation, represents this intent to find a new language that is able to recognize Others in their otherness through a process of cultural and social resurrection.

d. The "Pneumatological Turn": The Spirit "Fountain of Life"

The metaphorical resurrection of others and the new language for describing this process of flourishing as the vocation of every life depends on a new protagonist: the Holy Spirit. The "pneumatological turn" is the recognition of the Spirit, not as an ethical agent of holiness or discipline but as the fountain of life. This pneumatological renewal must not arouse suspicion in culture beyond the just and legitimate verification that must be exercised on every cultural new proposal. The introduction of pneumatology as the center of a new culture of life doesn't represent a hidden way of imposing a theological category on culture. Culture, as such, without passing through religion, even less through ecclesiological "confessions," is already a manifestation of the true Spirit. This cultural, nondenominational dimension of life is already a register of the Spirit in its inclusive universality. This inclusive universality of pneumatology is underlined in the most recent studies on pneumatology.[98]

In a context such as ours, theological and hermeneutical revival necessarily passes through the articulation of a "pneumatology of life."[99] The Spirit only transiently contains, disciplines, orders, restrains, and subdues. Its principal thrust is that of expanding, opening, motivating, imagining,

---

98. See Studebaker, *From Pentecost*, 214–16; Althouse, *Spirit of the Last Days*, 162–78.

99. This "pneumatology of life" can also be described as the maternal side of the Spirit in a clear alternative reading of the Trinity, as Maria Zambrano does, for example, in a philosophical–theological key when she speaks of the "femininity of the Spirit." Zambrano, *Cartas de la pièce*, 107. In this recovery of the feminine side of the Spirit, Zambrano relates to the work of Clement Alexandrinus, who believed that the Christian God, out of love for the world, also became a maternal God. Indeed, Clement Alexandrinus writes, "And while the ineffability of him is Father, compassion toward us has become mother. The Father because he loved, became feminine." Alessandrino, *Quale ricco si salverà?*, 37. See also, on Zambrano, Vantini, *Luce della perla*, 49–59.

breaking down limits, barriers, and obstacles in the flourishing of every life. The Spirit is sharing, bonding, communion, and commitment for life. The Spirit is the Spirit of life.[100] It is connected to life beyond words. Not that words do not express life; they do express it and mightily so, but the life expressed by the Spirit is often ineffable, that is, expressible only beyond words. This is because the Spirit of life does not express itself only on a human level. It exists beyond humans in all nonverbal communication.

This is the meaning of Bernard Sesboüé's reflection on the Holy Spirit. He conceives of the Holy Spirit as the Spirit of life. It is a "faceless and voiceless" Spirit because it is universally inclusive of all kinds of life. The Spirit's purpose is not so much to speak but to make others speak. Sesboüé writes,

> However, the proper role of the Spirit is not to speak of Himself but to make men whom He inspires speak according to the thought of the Father and the Son.[101]

CONCLUSION

The strong ecological metaphor of the tree, the center and beating heart of Ps 1, cannot and should not be swallowed up by the impetuousness and dragging force of the model of the mobile and dynamic believer. To the "fast-faith" (fast-food) of the performative model, this psalm contrasts the wisdom, inclusiveness, and freshness of the "slow-faith" (slow-food) model of the tree that is still and unmoving, but precisely for this reason is able to transmit life through its bountiful fruit. But slow faith, presupposed by the tree model, is such by virtue of complexity and heterogeneity that only that kind of faith can unveil. As Emanuele Coccia says, "the self is a forest,"[102] and like the tree in the midst of a forest, I can only see and understand it if I slow my pace, indeed if I stop and take roots in the ground I'm standing on. Only if I become like a tree can I really understand a tree. Only those who stand still can understand a still life. But to learn to stand still, a sporadic prescription is not enough (see Ps 46:10). What is needed is a sustained educational path over time, which Luigina Mortari describes as a true

---

100. Moltmann, *Spirito della vita*, 120–45. See also Congar, *Credo nello Spirito Santo*, 34–45.
101. Sesboüé, *Spirito senza volto*, 15.
102. Coccia, "Io è una foresta," 9–22.

"ecological education" to anthropological slowness through relations.[103] Criteria that determine the profile of an educational offer do not disappear but are certainly reversed. Autonomy, as the main and primordial goal of education, no longer subsists as such but is replaced by the model of human and ecological relationship, in which autonomy and dependence create an irreducible structural tension that guarantees life and flourishing.

Psalm 1 pushes us to face some crucial questions: What does it mean to be a witness to life and not just be concerned about the order or linearity of successful events in our experience? Why do we prefer the fast language of concepts to the slow language of metaphors? How does it become possible to destroy ourselves and others around us with things that are formally right but that we deform with our compulsion to haste and time? Why do we often confuse instruments that help us live with life itself? How do we become in time the source and cause of our own alienation and destruction? Why is it so difficult to rely on vulnerability and incompleteness in our existential and religious journey?

Psalm 1 reminds us that the more noble and consistent human experience is not that of quantity, speed, size, and heroic resilience but rather that of trust, relationships, and vulnerable and fragile flourishing. The understanding of this fundamental anthropological truth is sometimes more important than some doctrinal and ethical refined elaborations because a muscular understanding of life has invaded our families and pushes us to think of family well-being only in terms of professional, physical, and financial success and functionality. Our families are hurting not because they do not achieve the minimal goals imposed by society but rather because they often achieve them without being able to create that refreshing air of an authentic, vulnerable, and inclusive life embodied in ongoing, slow, and long-breathing relationships. The metaphor of the tree reminds us of the importance and value of life over the necessary norms created to preserve it. Often, very often, a worthy life reveals itself to us as a slow, still, halved, and threatened life. For this reason, we should remember that not everything that moves necessarily conveys life, just as not everything that is still is necessarily dead. It may be just the opposite, as this psalm tries to demonstrate. The tree standing still is open to a welcoming time that is not linear but an interrupted time because it is a time contaminated with presences, words, silences, uncertainties, and wonders of people who think of themselves and their own thinking as incomplete and partial. As Italian

103. Mortari, *Educazione ecologica*, 74–91.

poetess Chandra Candiani reminds us, only the perception and awareness of our "immense not knowing" can put us back in the track of life understood as relation, communion, trust and flourishing.[104]

---

104. Candiani, *Questo immenso non sapere*, 12–35.

Conclusion

A "slow Adventism" implies something more than simply slowing down the speed of what we do and what we say. It implies a harder exercise that requires a revisitation of what we are and what we think in the light of a cultural context of which we are often not aware. A context that is not completely bad or good, and for this reason demands from us discernment, humility, foresight, discipline, courage, and conviction. Implicitly and indirectly, we hope these pages represent an encouragement to know, to study, and to reflect on our culture as much as we do with the Bible. In medicine, it's not enough to know the medical strategies for healing if we ignore the human specificities of the patient who aspires to be healed. In the same way, knowing the Bible alone as remedy for humanity is not enough if we don't understand the human we want to help, who is always rooted in a specific sociocultural context.

A full and rapid life is paradoxically an endangered life. It hides within itself the seed of its own destruction. This is why the rush to be complete is one of the worst aspirations we may ever have. It makes us not only self-sufficient, happy with ourselves, it also kills in us the desire for others. Bulimia and obesity are not only person-related eating disorders. They have parallel cultural and religious forms that often go undiagnosed and are the precursors and facilitators of those individual psychological dysfunctionalities we all know. Today, churches, as much as their parallel societies they interact with, are culturally and theologically obese systems in urgent need of incompleteness and vulnerability.

So, "slow Adventism" simply means the search of a reasonable Adventism that focuses on quality, not only on quantity. Losing some religious weight and discovering the value of theological incompleteness and

Conclusion

vulnerability may help us be more empathic and enhance the value of the mission we have received for today's world. Plethoric bodies are less resistant. Vulnerable bodies are more resistant and resilient. Making Adventism "slow and reasonable" is a kenotic process. Not muscular, heroic, and bold affirmations but vulnerable, sober, and emphatic witnessing can put Adventism back on the track of life.

Bibliography

Acemoglu, Daron, and James A. Robinson. *Why Nations Fail: The Origins of Power, Prosperity, and Poverty*. London: Profile, 2013.

Alessandrino, C. *Quale ricco si salverà?* [What rich man will be saved?]. Rome: Città Nuova, 1999.

Althouse, Peter. *Spirit of the Last Days: Pentecostal Eschatology in Conversation with Jürgen Moltmann*. London: T&T Clark International, 2003.

Appiah, Kwame Anthony. *The Ethics of Identity*. Princeton, NJ: Princeton University Press, 2005.

Arendt, Hannah. *The Human Condition*. Chicago: Chicago University Press, 1998.

———. *Vita activa. La condizione umana*. Translated by Sergio Finzi. Milan: Bompiani, 2008.

Arguedas, José María. *I fiumi profondi* [Deep rivers]. Translated by Umberto Bonetti. Turin, IT: Einaudi, 2011.

Aristotle. *The Nicomachean Ethics*. Translated by J. A. K. Thomson. London: Penguin, 2004.

Augé, Marc. *Non-luoghi: Introduzione ad una antropologia della surmodernità*. Edited by Dominique Rolland and Carlo Milani. Milan: Eleuthera, 2005.

———. *Non-Places: An Introduction to Supermodernity*. Translated by John Howe. New York: Verso, 2009.

Austin, J. L. *How to Do Things with Words*. Eastford, CT: Martino Fine, 2014.

Balthasar, Hans Urs Von. *The Glory of God: A Theological Aesthetics*. 7 vols. San Francisco: Ignatius, 1982.

Benasayag, Miguel, and Angélique Del Rey. *Elogio del conflitto* [The praise of conflict]. Translated by Frederico Leoni. Milano: Feltrinelli, 2008.

Benasayag, Miguel, and Gérard Schmit. *L'epoca delle passioni tristi* [The season of sad passions]. Translated by Eleanora Missana. Milan: Feltrinelli, 2005.

Benedict, Ruth. *The Chrysanthemum and the Sword: Patterns of Japanese Culture*. Boston: Mariner, 2006.

Benhabib, Seyla. "The Elusiveness of the Particular: Hannah Arendt, Walter Benjamin, and Theodor Adorno." In *Exile, Statelessness, and Migration: Playing Chess with History from Hannah Arendt to Isaiah Berlin*, 34–60. Princeton, NJ: Princeton University Press, 2018.

Bibliography

Benjamin, Walter. *The Arcades Project*. Cambridge, MA: Belknap, 2002.

———. "Thesis on the Philosophy of History." In *Illuminations: Essays and Reflections*, 196–208. Boston: Mariner, 2019.

Bhabha, Homi K. *The Location of Culture*. London: Routledge, 2007.

Bielik-Robson, Agata, ed. *Another Finitude: Messianic Vitalism and Philosophy*. London: Bloomsbury Academic, 2020.

Bielik-Robson, Agata, and Daniel H. Weiss, eds. *Tsimtsum and Modernity: Lurianic Heritage in Modern Philosophy and Theology*. Berlin: De Gruyter, 2020.

Bobbio, Norberto. *Elogio della mitezza*. Milan: Il Saggiatore, 1998.

Böckenförde, Ernst-Wolfgang. *La formazione dello Stato come processo di secolarizzazione* [The formation of the state as a process of secularization]. Translated by Corrado Bertani. Brescia, IT: Morcelliana, 2005.

Bodei, Remo. *La vita delle cose* [The life of things]. Rome: Laterza, 2011.

Bollas, Christopher. *Meaning and Melancholia: Life in the Age of Bewilderment*. New York: Routledge, 2018.

Brueggemann, Walter. *The Message of the Psalms: A Theological Commentary*. Minneapolis: Augsburg, 1984.

Brueggemann, Walter, and William H. Bellinger Jr. *Psalms*. New York: Cambridge University Press, 2014.

Butler, Judith. "Grievability for the Living." In *What World Is This? A Pandemic Phenomenology*, 88–99. New York: Columbia University Press, 2022.

Cacciari, Massimo. *Paradiso e naufragio: Saggio su L'uomo senza qualità* [Paradise and shipwreck: Essay on Musil's man without qualities]. Turin, IT: Einaudi, 2022.

Caffo, Leonardo. *Fragile umanità: Il postumano contemporaneo* [Fragile humanity: Contemporary post-humanism]. Turin, IT: Einaudi, 2017.

Calvino, Italo. *Six Memos for the Next Millennium*. Translated by Geoffrey Brock. London: Penguin Classics, 2009.

Candiani, Chandra. *Sogni de fiume* [River dreams]. Turin, IT: Einaudi, 2022.

———. *Questo immenso non sapere. Conversazioni con alberi, animali e il cuore umano* [This immense not knowing: Conversations with trees, animals, and the human heart]. Turin, IT: Einaudi, 2021.

Casey, Edward S. *The Fate of Place. A Philosophical History*. Oakland, CA: University of California Press, 1998.

Castro-Gómez, Santiago, and Ramón Grosfoguel, eds. *Il giro decolonial: Reflexiones para una diversidad epistémica más allá del capitalismo global*. Bogotá, CO: Siglo del Hombre, 2007.

Cavarero, Adriana. *Inclinations: A Critique of Rectitude*. Translated by Adam Sitze and Amanda Minervini. Stanford: Stanford University Press, 2016.

Chicchi, Federico, and Anna Simone. *La società della prestazione* [The achievement society]. Rome: Ediesse, 2017.

Celidwen, Yuria. *Flourishing Kin: Indigenous Wisdom for Collective Well-Being*. Louisville, CO: Sounds True, 2024.

Coccia, Emanuele. *Matamorfosi. Siamo un'unica, sola vita* [Metamorphosis: We are one, single life]. Turin, IT: Einaudi, 2022.

———. "Prefazione all'edzione italiana: L'io è una foresta" [Preface to the Italian edition: The self is a forest]. In *Come pensano le foreste: Per un'antropologia oltre l'umano* [How forests think: Toward an anthropology beyond the human] by Eduardo Kohn,

Bibliography

9–22. Translated by Alessandro Lucera and Alessandro Palmieri. Milan: Nottetempo, 2021.

Collins, John J. *Introduction to the Hebrew Bible*. Minneapolis: Fortress, 2014.

Congar, Yves. *Credo nello Spirito santo*. Brescia, IT: Queriniana, 1979.

Cortina, Adela. *Aporofobia, el rechazo al pobre: Un desafío para la democracia* [Aporophobia, the exclusion of the poor: A challenge for democracy]. Barcelona: Paidós, 2019.

De La Torre, Miguel Angel. *Embracing Hopelessness*. Minneapolis: Fortress, 2017.

Di Ceglie, Roberto. *God, the Good, and the Spiritual Turn in Epistemology*. Cambridge: Cambridge University Press, 2023.

Dufourmantelle, Anne. *La potenza della dolcezza* [The power of sweetness]. Translated by Mario Porro. Milan: Vita e Pensiero, 2013.

Eagleton, Terry. *Hope Without Optimism*. New Haven, CT: Yale University Press, 2019.

Ehrenberg, Alan. *The Weariness of the Self: Diagnosing the History of Depression in the Contemporary Age*. Montreal: McGill Queens University Press, 2009.

———. *The Worship of Performance*. Paris: Hachette, 2011.

Esposito, Roberto. *Le persone e le cose* [Persons and things]. Turin, IT: Einaudi, 2014.

Esquirol, Josep Maria. *Humà, més humà: Una antropologia de la ferida infinita* [Human, more human: An anthropology of the infinite wound]. Barcelona: Institut Ramon Llull, 2021.

Fanon, Frantz. *The Wretched of the Earth*. London: Penguin Classics, 2001.

Floridi, Luciano. *Pensare l'infosfera. La filosofia come design concettuale* [Thinking the infosphere: Philosophy as conceptual design]. Turin, IT: Bollati Boringhieri, 2020.

Flusser, Vilém. *La cultura dei media* [The culture of the media]. Milan: Bruno Mondadori, 2004.

Fodor, Jerry Alan. *The Modularity of Mind*. Cambridge: MIT Press, 1992.

Forte, Bruno. *Dove va il cristianesimo?* [Where is Christianity going?] Brescia, IT: Queriniana, 2001.

Freud, Sigmund. *Beyond the Pleasure Principle*. New York: Dover, 2015.

Frisby, David. *Fragments of Modernity: Theories of Modernity in the Work of Simmel, Kracauer, and Benjamin*. London: Routledge, 1986.

Fromm, Erich. *The Art of Loving*. New York: Harper, 2019.

———. *The Heart of Man: Its Genius for Good and Evil*. New York: Harper, 1992.

Fuchs, Thomas. "The Cyclical Time of the Body and the Linear Time of Modernity." In *In Defense of the Human Being: Foundational Questions of an Embodied Anthropology*, 217–30. Oxford: Oxford University Press, 2021.

Galimberti, Umberto. *Il tramonto dell'Occidente nella lettura di Heidegger e Jaspers* [The decline of the west in the thought of Heidegger and Jaspers]. Milan: Feltrinelli, 2009.

Geffré, Claude. *Credere e interpretare. La svolta ermeneutica della teologia*. Brescia, IT: Queriniana, 2002.

Giddens, Anthony. *The Consequences of Modernity*. Stanford: Stanford University Press, 1994.

Ginzburg, Carlo. *Threads and Traces: True, False, Fictive*. Oakland, CA: University of California Press, 2012.

Goldberg, Arnold. *The Problem of Perversion*. New Haven, CT: Yale University Press, 1998.

Gourevitch, Aaron Y. "Postface: Le temps comme problème d'histoire culturelle." In *Les cultures et les temps*, edited by Paul Ricoeur, 257–76. Paris: Payot, 1975.

Gramsci, Antonio. *Quaderni del carcere* [Letters from Prison]. Turin, IT: Einaudi, 2014.

Bibliography

Gunkel, Herman, and Joachim Begrich. *Einleitung in die Psalmen: Die Gattungen der Religiösen Lyrik Israel*. Göttingen, DE: Vandenhoeck & Ruprecht, 1933.

Gutierrez Salazar, Hanz. *Beyond the Bible, Beyond the West: The "Eros" of Interpretation*. Milan: Mimesis, 2024.

———. "A Spatial Theology of the Sabbath (Part 4)—A World of Living Things." *Spectrum Magazine*, Feb. 13, 2020. https://spectrummagazine.org/views/spatial-theology-sabbath-part-4-world-living-things/.

———. "A Spatial Theology of the Sabbath: Temporal Alienation (Part 3)." *Spectrum Magazine*, Oct. 10, 2019. https://spectrummagazine.org/views/spatial-theology-sabbath-temporal-alienation-part-3/.

———. "A Spatial Theology of the Sabbath: The Disenchantment of Place (Part 2)." *Spectrum Magazine*, Sept. 12, 2019. https://spectrummagazine.org/views/spatial-theology-sabbath-part-ii-disenchantment-place/.

———. "A Spatial Theology of the Sabbath: Time over Space? (Part 1)." *Spectrum Magazine*, Aug. 18, 2019. https://spectrummagazine.org/views/spatial-theology-sabbath-time-over-space-part-1/.

Habermas, Jürgen. *The Inclusion of the Other: Studies in Political Theory*. Edited by Ciaran P. Cronin and Pablo de Greiff. Cambridge, MA: MIT Press, 1998.

———. *Religion and Rationality: Essays on Reason, God, and Modernity*. Edited by Eduardo Mendieta. London: Polity, 2002.

Haidt, Jonathan. *The Happiness Hypothesis: Finding Modern Truth in Ancient Wisdom*. New York: Basic Books, 2006.

Han, Byung-Chul. "Beyond Disciplinary Society." In *The Burnout Society*, 8–11. Stanford: Stanford University Press, 2015.

———. *Eros in agonia* [The agony of eros]. Translated by Frederica Buongiorno. Milan: NotteTempo, 2012.

———. *La società senza dolore: Perché abbiamo bandito la sofferenza* [Algo-Phobic Society: Why We Have Banished Suffering from Our Lives]. Translated by Simone Aglan-Buttazzi. Turin, IT: Einaudi, 2021.

———. *Le non cose: Come abbiamo smesso di vivere il reale* [Non-things: Upheaval in the lifeworld]. Translated by Simone Aglan-Buttazzi. Turin, IT: Einaudi, 2022.

———. *L'espulsione dell'altro* [The exclusion of the other]. Translated by Vittorio Tamaro. Milan: Nottetempo, 2016.

Haraway, Donna. *Simians, Cyborgs, and Women: The Reinvention of Nature*. New York: Routledge, 1991.

Haraway, Donna, and Adele Clarke, eds. *Making Kin Not Population*. Chicago: Prickly Paradigm, 2018.

Hegel, Georg Wilhelm Fredrich. *Elements of the Philosophy of Right*. Cambridge: Cambridge University Press, 1991.

Heidegger, Martin. *Eraclito* [Heraclitus]. Translated by Franco Camera. Milan: Mursia, 2020.

———. *Holzwege*. Frankfurt am Main, DE: Vittorio Klostermann, 2015.

Hesse, Herman. *Siddhartha*. Translated by M. Mila. Milan: Adelphi, 1990.

Hillman, James. *Re-Visioning Psychology*. New York: Harper, 1992.

Hobbes, Thomas. *De cive. Elementi filosofici sul cittadino* [On the citizen: Philosophical elements on the citizen]. Edited by Tito Magri. Rome: Editori Riuniti, 2014.

———. *Leviatano* [Leviathan]. Translated by Gianni Micheli. Milan: Rizzoli, 2013.

Bibliography

Honneth, Axel. *Verdinglichung: Eine anerkennungstheoretische Studie*. Berlin: Suhrkamp, 2015.
Illouz, Eva. *Cold Intimacies: The Making of Emotional Capitalism*. Cambridge: Polity, 2007.
Inge, John. *A Christian Theology of Place*. London: Routledge, 2016.
Kierkegaard, Søren. *Fear and Trembling*. Translated by Alastair Hannay. London: Penguin Classics, 2011.
———. *The Sickness unto Death: A Christian Psychological Exposition for Edification and Awakening by Anti-Climacus*. Translated by Alastair Hannay. London: Penguin, 2004.
Knight, George R. *A Search for Identity: The Development of Seventh-Day Adventist Beliefs*. Hagerstown, MD: Review and Herald, 2000.
Kohn, Eduardo. *Come pensano le foreste: Per un'antropologia oltre l'umano* [How forests think: Toward an anthropology beyond the human]. Translated by Alessandro Lucera and Alessandro Palmieri. Milan: Nottetempo, 2021.
Koselleck, Reinhardt. *Futuro passato: Per una semantica dei tempi storici* [Past future: For a semantic of historical times]. Bologna, IT: Clueb, 2007.
Kundera, Milan. *The Art of the Novel*. New York: Grove, 1988.
———. *The Unbearable Lightness of Being*. London: Faber & Faber, 1988.
Lacan, Jacques. *The Ethics of Psychoanalysis*. The Seminar of Jaques Lacan: Book VII. London: Routledge, 1992.
Lancellotti, Angelo. *I salmi* [The Psalms]. Milan: Edzione Paoline, 1995.
LaRondelle, Hans K. *Perfection and Perfectionism: A Dogmatic-Ethical Study of Biblical Perfection and Phenomenal Perfectionism*. Berrien Spring, MI: Andrews University Press, 1975.
Lebrecht, N. *Why Mahler: How One Man and Ten Symphonies Changed the World*. London: Faber & Faber, 2011.
Lipovetsky, Gilles. *L'ère du vide. Essais sur l'individualisme contemporain*. Paris: Gallimard, 1993.
MacIntyre, Alasdair. *After Virtue: A Study in Moral Theory*. Notre Dame: University of Notre Dame Press, 1984.
Maffei, Lamberto. *Elogio della lentezza* [In praise of slowness]. Bologna, IT: Il Mulino, 2014.
Mamani, Fernando Huanacuni. *Vivir bien/Buen vivir. Filosofía, políticas, estrategias y experiencias de los pueblos ancestrales*. Lima: CAOI, 2010.
Mancuso, Stefano. *Plant Revolution: Le piante hanno già inventato il nostro futuro* [Plant Revolution: Plants have already invented our future]. Florence: Giunti, 2017.
Mancuso, Stefano, and Alessandra Viola. *Verde brillante: Sensibilità e intelligenza del mondo vegetale* [Brilliant green: The surprising history and science of plant intelligence]. Florence: Giunti, 2019.
Margulis, Lynn. *Symbiotic Planet: A New Look at Evolution*. New York: Basic Books, 1999.
Marramao, Giacomo. *Kairos: Apologia del tempo debito* [Kairos: Apology of due time]. Turin, IT: Bollati Boringhieri, 2020.
———. *The Passage West: Philosophy After the Age of the Nation State*. Translated by Matteo Mandarini. New York: Verso, 2012.
———. *La passione del presente. Breve lessico della modernità-mondo* [Passion for the present: Short lexicon of the modernity-world]. Turin, IT: Bollati Boringhieri, 2008.
Mays, James L. *Psalms*. Louisville, KY: Westminster John Knox, 2011.
McGibbon, Elizabeth A., ed. *Oppression: A Social Determinant of Health*. Halifax, CA: Fernwood, 2021.

Bibliography

McWilliams, Nancy. *Psychoanalytic Diagnosis: Understanding Personality Structure in the Clinical Process*. New York: Guilford, 2011.

Medina, Javier. *Suma Qamaña. Por una convivialidad postindustrial*. La Paz, BO: Ministerio de Hacienda, 2000.

Miller, Darrow L., and Gary Brumbelow. *Wisdom: The Way to Human Flourishing*. Seattle, WA: YWAM Publishing, 2019.

Milo, Daniel S. *Good Enough: The Tolerance for Mediocrity in Nature and Society*. Cambridge, MA: Harvard University Press, 2019.

Moltmann, Jurgen. *The Coming God: Christian Eschatology*. Translated by Margaret Kohl. Minneapolis: Fortress, 2004.

———. *L'avvento di Dio. Escatologia cristiana*. Translated by D. Pezzetta. Brescia, IT: Queriniana, 1998.

———. *Lo spirito della vita: Per una pneumatologia integrale*. Translated by D. Pezzetta. Brescia, IT: Queriniana, 1994.

———. *Trinità e Regno di Dio*. Translated by D. Pezzetta. Brescia, IT: Queriniana, 2020.

Montaigne, Michel de. *Saggi* [Essays]. Edited by Fausta Garavini and André Turnon. Milan: Bonpiani, 2014.

Mortari, Luigina. *Educazione ecologica* [Ecological education]. Rome: Laterza, 2020.

Mouffe, Chantal. *Agonistics: Thinking the World Politically*. London: Verso, 2013.

———. *The Democratic Paradox*. London: Verso, 2000.

Mouffe, Chantal, and Ernesto Laclau. *Hegemony and Social Strategy: Toward a Radical Democratic Politics*. New York: Verso, 2001.

Mounk, Yascha. *The Identity Trap: A Story of Ideas and Power in Our Time*. London: Penguin, 2023.

Natoli, Salvatore. *La felicità saggio di teoria degli affetti* [Happiness: Essay on a theory of affection]. Milan: Feltrinelli, 2007.

Ngomane, Mungi. *Everyday Ubuntu: Living Better Together, the African Way*. London: Penguin Random House, 2019.

Nietzsche, Friedrich. *The Birth of Tragedy: Out of The Spirit of Music*. London: Penguin, 2001.

———. *La gaia scienza e idilli di Messina* [The gay science and idylls of Messina]. Translated by Ferruccio Masini. Milan: Adelphi, 1977.

———. *Twilight of the Idols or How to Philosophize with a Hammer*. Oxford: Oxford University Press, 2002.

Nussbaum, Martha. *The Fragility of Goodness: Luck and Ethics in Greek Tragedy and Philosophy*. Cambridge: Cambridge University Press, 2013.

———. *L'intelligenza delle emozioni* [Upheavals of Thought]. Translated by R. Scognamiglio. Bologna, IT: Il Mulino, 2004.

Oz, Amos. *Contro il fanatismo* [How to cure a fanatic]. Translated by E. Loewenthal. Milan: Feltrinelli, 2015.

Pannenberg, Wolfhart. *Grundlagen der Ethik: Philosophisch-theologische Perspektiven*. Göttingen: Vandenhoeck & Ruprecht, 2004.

Paz, Octavio. *El ogro filantrópico: Historia y política, 1971–1978* [The philanthropic ogre: History and politics 1971–1978]. Ciudad de México: Joaquin Moritz, 1979.

Pellegrino, Gianfranco, and Marcello Di Paola. *Etica e politica delle piante* [Ethics and politics of plants]. Rome: Derive Approdi, 2019.

Perdue, Leo G. *Wisdom and Creation: The Theology of Wisdom Literature*. Eugene, OR: Wipf & Stock, 1994.

Bibliography

Piketty, Thomas. *The Capital in the Twenty-First Century*. Cambridge, MA: Harvard University Press, 2014.

Prigogine, Ilya. *The End of Certainty: Time, Chaos, and the New Laws of Nature*. New York: Free Press, 1997.

Pulcini, Elena. *Tra cura e giustizia. Le passioni come risorsa sociale* [Between care and justice: Passions as social resources]. Turin, IT: Bollati Boringhieri, 2020.

———. *The Individual Without Passions: Modern Individualism and the Loss of the Social Bond*. New York: Lexington, 2012.

Rafele, Antonio. *La Métropole: Benjamin et Simmel* [Metropolis: Benjamin and Simmel]. Paris: CNRS, 2010.

Ramelli, Illaria L. E. *The Christian Doctrine of Apokatastasis: A Critical Assessment from the New Testament to Eriugena*. Leiden, NL: Brill, 2013.

Ratzinger, Joseph, and Jürgen Habermas. *Etica, religione e stato liberale* [Ethics, religion and the liberal state]. Translated by Giulio Colombi and Omar Brino. Brescia, IT: Morcelliana, 2005.

Ravasi, Gianfranco. *Salmi. Introduzione, testo e commento* [The Psalms: Introduction]. *Text and Commentary*. Milan: St. Paul, 2006.

Recalcati, Massimo. *Elogio dell'inconscio. Dodici argomenti in difesa della psicoanalisi* [In praise of the unconscious: Twelve arguments in defense of psychoanalysis]. Milan: Mondadori, 2007.

———. *La legge del desiderio. Radici bibliche della psicoanalisi* [The law of desire: Biblical roots of psychoanalysis]. Turin: Einaudi, 2024.

Ribeyro, Julio Ramón. *La tentación del fracaso* [The temptation of failing]. Lima: Planeta, 2019.

Rice, Richard. *Believing, Behaving, Belonging: Finding New Love for the Church*. Roseville, CA: Association of Adventist Forums, 2002.

Ricœur, Paul. *Ermeneutica filosofica ed ermeneutica biblica*. Translated by Attilio Sottili. Turin, IT: Claudiana, 2021.

———. *Oneself as Another*. Chicago: Chicago University Press, 1992.

Rivera, Mayra. *The Touch of Transcendence. A Postcolonial Theology of God*. Louisville, KY: Westminster John Knox, 2007.

Rodotà, Stefano. *La vita e le regole: Tra diritto e non-diritto*. Milan: Feltrinelli, 2018.

Rosa, Hartmut. *Alienation and Acceleration: Towards a Critical Theory of Late-Modern Temporality*. Aarhus, DK: Aarhus University Press, 2010.

———. "If Our Problem Is Acceleration, Can 'Resonance' Be the Solution? The Crisis of Dynamic Stabilization and the Perspective of a Critic of the Present." *Annali di Studi Religiosi* 18 (2017) 7–36.

Rovelli, Carlo. *Che cos'è il tempo? Che cos'è lo spazio?* [What is time? What is space?] Rome: Di Renzo Editore, 2014.

Roy, Olivier. *L'appiattimento del mondo: La crisi della cultura e il dominio della norma* [The flattening of the world: The crisis of culture and the dominion of the norm]. Translated by Massimiliano Guareschi. Milan: Feltrinelli, 2024.

Said, Edward W. *Orientalism*. London: Penguin Classics, 2003.

Schleiermacher, Friedrich. *On Religion: Speeches to Its Cultured Despisers*. Cambridge: Cambridge University Press, 1996.

Scholem, Gershom. *Concetti fondamentali dell'ebraismo* [Fundamental categories of Hebraism]. Translated by Michele Bertaggia. Milan: Marietti 1820, 1986.

———. *Die jüdische Mystik in ihren Hauptströmungen*. Frankfurt, DE: Suhrkamp, 2009.

Bibliography

———. *Schöpfung aus Nichts und Selbstverschränkung Gottes*. Ascona, CH: Eranos-Jahrbuch, 1956.
Schopenhauer, Arthur. *The World as Will and Representation*. Cambridge: Cambridge University Press, 2020.
Scott, Jordan. *Io parlo come un fiume* [I talk like a river]. Rome: Orecchio Acerbo, 2021.
Sesboüé, Bernard. *Lo Spirito senza volto e senza voce: Breve storia della teologia dello Spirito Santo*. Milan: San Paolo, 2010.
Simmel, Georg. *Le metropoli e la vita dello spirito* [The metropolis and the mental life]. Rome: Armando Editore, 2013.
———. *On Individuality and Social Forms*. Chicago: Chicago University Press, 1971.
Sloterdijk, Peter. *Bubbles: Spheres I*. Translated by Wieland Hoban. Los Angeles: Semiotext(e), 2011.
———. *Foams: Spheres III*. Translated by Wieland Hoban. Los Angeles: Semiotext(e), 2016.
———. *Globes: Spheres II*. Translated by Wieland Hoban. Los Angeles: Semiotext(e), 2014.
———. *Grigio. Il colore della contemporaneità* [Gray: The Color of Our Contemporary World]. Translated by Gianluca Bonaiuti. Florence: Marsilio Editori, 2023.
———. *Kritik der Zynischen Vernunft*. Frankfurt: Suhrkamp, 1988.
Solon, Pablo. *¿Es posible el Vivir Bien? Reflexiones a Quema Ropa sobre Alternativas Sistemicas*. La Paz, BO: Solon, 2016.
Spengler, Oswald. *The Decline of the West: Form and Actuality*. Budapest: Arktos, 2021.
Spinoza, Benedict. *Ethics*. London: Penguin, 1996.
Spivak, Gayatri Chakravorty, and Judith Butler. *Who Sings the Nation-State? Language, Politics, Belonging*. London: Seagull, 2015.
Studebaker, Steven M. *From Pentecost to the Triune God: A Pentecostal Trinitarian Theology*. Grand Rapids: Eerdmans, 2012.
Taylor, Charles. *The Malaise of Modernity*. Toronto: House of Anansi, 2024.
———. *A Secular Age*. Cambridge, MA: Harvard University Press, 2007.
Tönnies, Ferdinand. *Gemeinschaft und Gesellschaft*. Berlin: Springer, 2004.
Tonstad, Linn Marie. *Queer Theology: Beyond Apologetics*. Eugene, OR: Cascade, 2018.
Tocqueville, Alexis de. *Democracy in America*. Translated by Harvey C. Mansfield and Delba Winthrop. New York: Barnes & Noble, 2003.
Trías, Eugenio. *Pensar la religión* [Thinking religion]. Barcelona: Galaxia Gutenberg, 2015.
Vahanian, Gabriel. *The Death of God: The Culture of Our Post-Christian Era*. New York: George Braziller, 1961.
Vantini, Lucia. *La luce della perla. La scrittura di Maria Zambrano tra filosofia e teologia* [The light of the pearl: Maria Zambrano's writing between philosophy and theology]. Cantalupa, IT: Effatà Editrice, 2008.
Von Rad, Gerhard. *Weisheit in Israel*. Neukirchen, DE: Gütersloher, 1990.
Waldenfels, Bernhard. *Estraneo, straniero, straordinario. Saggi di fenomenologia responsiva* [Stranger, foreigner, extraordinary: Essays in responsive phenomenology]. Edited by Ugo Perone. Turin, IT: Rosenberg & Sellier, 2020.
———. *Grundmotive einer Phänomenologie des Fremdes*. Frankfurt am Main: Suhrkamp, 2018.
———. *Studien zur Phänomenologie des Fremdes*. vols. 1–4. Berlin: Suhrkamp, 2016.
———. *Topographie des Fremdes*. Studien zur Phänomenologie des Fremdes 1. Berlin: Suhrkamp, 2016.

Bibliography

Walker-Jones, Arthur. *The Green Psalter: Resources for an Ecological Spirituality.* Minneapolis: Fortress, 2009.
Weber, Andreas. *Indigenialität.* Berlin: NP & I, 2018.
Weber, Max. *Economy and Society.* Cambridge, MA: Harvard University Press, 2019.
———. *Politik als Beruf.* Frankfurt: Anaconda Verlag, 2005.
———.*The Protestant Ethic and the Spirit of Capitalism.* London: Routledge, 2021.
———. *The Sociology of Religion.* Translated by Ephraim Fischoff. Boston: Beacon, 1992.
Westermann, Claus. *Praise and Lament in the Psalms.* Atlanta: John Knox, 1981.
White, Ellen G. *Christ's Object Lessons.* Hagerstown, MD: Review and Herald, 1991.
———. *Education.* Hagerstown, MD: Review and Herald, 1976.
Yao, Joanne. *The Ideal River: How Control of Nature Shaped International Order.* Manchester: Manchester University Press, 2021.
Zambrano, Maria. *Cartas de la Pièce. Correspondencia con Augustin Andreu.* Valencia: Universidad Politècnica de Valencia, 2002.
Zaoui, Pierre. *L'arte di essere felici. Come sopravvivere alle avversità e riscoprire il valore della vita* [The Art of Being Happy: How to Overcome Adversities and Discover the Value of Life]. Translated by Cecilia Pirovano. Milan: Il Saggiatore, 2016.
———. *L'arte di scomparire. Vivere con discrezione* [The Art of Disappearing: Live with Discretion]. Translated by A. Guareschi. Milan: Il Saggiatore, 2015.
Zehou, Li. *The Humanist Ethics.* New York: State University of New York Press, 2023.
Zoja, Luigi. *La morte del prossimo* [The death of the neighbor]. Turin, IT: Einaudi, 2018.

Author Index

Acemoglu, Daron, 66, 88, 89
Adorno, Theodor, 42
Althouse, Peter, 158
Appiah, Kwame A., 53
Arguedas, Jose M., 10
Arendt, Hannah, 20, 42, 150
Aristotle, 110
Augé, Marc, 151
Austin, John L., 5

Barth, Karl, 29
Bellinger, H.William, 4, 118
Benasayag, Miguel, 95, 100, 101
Benedict, Ruth, 18
Benhabib, Seyla, 42
Benjamin, Walter, 18, 23, 42
Bentham Jeremy, 130
Bhabha, Homi K., 14
Bielik-Robson, Agata, 127
Bobbio, Norberto, 107
Bodei, Remo, 150
Bollas, Christopher, 51, 62, 142, 146
Borghini, Vincenzo, 115
Böckenförde, Ernst-Wolfgang, 77
Brueggemann, Walter, 4, 118, 124
Butler, Judith, 7, 44

Calvino, Italo, 43
Caffo, Leonardo, 112
Cacciari, Massimo, 145
Candiani, Chandra, 30, 161
Casey, Edward S., 37

Castro Gomez, Santiago, 33
Cavarero, Adriana, 61, 62
Celidwen, Yuria, 118, 120
Cervantes, Miguel, 46
Chicchi, Federico, 15, 23, 84
Coccia, Emmanuele, 112, 159
Collins, John J., 119
Cortina, Adela, 75

De La Torre, Miguel Angel, 101
De Tocqueville, Alexis, 107
Di Ceglie, Roberto, 156
Di Paola, Marcello, 133
Dufourmantelle, Anne, 99

Eagleton, Terry, 101
Ehrenberg, Alain, 142
Esposito, Roberto, 27, 139
Esquirol, Josep Maria, xviii, 74

Fanon, Frantz, 13
Floridi, Luciano, 152
Flusser, Vilem, 152
Fodor, Jerry A., 44
Forte, Bruno, 28
Freud, Sigmund, 144
Frisby, David, 23
Fromm, Erich, 19, 122, 136, 137, 149
Fuchs, Thomas, 59

Galimberti, Umberto, 142
Giddens, Anthony, 21

Author Index

Ginzburg, Carlo, 38
Goldberg, Arnold, 86
Gourevitch, Aaron Y., 15, 83
Gramsci, Antonio, 4, 5
Greffé, Claude, 156, 157
Gunkel, Hermann, 4, 118
Gutierrez Salazar, Hanz, 82, 139, 143

Haidt, Jonathan, 119, 130, 131
Han, Byung-Chul, 8, 16, 17, 45, 83, 85, 150, 152
Habermas, Jürgen, 74, 77, 78, 80
Haraway, Donna, 33, 111
Hegel, Friedrich, 36, 37, 66
Heidegger, Martin, 31
Heraclitus, 10
Hesse, Hermann, 30
Hillman, James, 63
Hobbes, Thomas, 11, 76, 77, 130
Honneth, Axel, 27, 136, 137, 145

Illouz, Elena, 23
Inge, John, 37

John Paul II, 105
Jones A. T., 96

Kierkegaard, Søren, 36, 49, 66, 134
Knight, Georges R., 96
Kohn, Eduardo, 134
Koselleck, Reinhardt, 100, 101
Kundera, Milan, 43, 44, 45, 46

Lacan, Jacques, 56, 57
Lancellotti, Angelo, 4, 118
LaRondelle, Hans K., 60
Lebrecht, Norman, 152
Leo XIII, 105
Lipovetsky, Gilles, 142
Locke, John, 130
Luria Isaac, 126
Luther Martin, 64

Maffei, Lamberto, 87
Mahler, Gustav, 152, 153, 154
Mamani Fernando, 119
Mancuso, Stefano, 134

Margulis, Lynn, 111
McWilliams, Nancy, 44, 146
Marramao, Giacomo, 15, 68, 151
Mays, L. James, 4, 118, 120
McGibbon, Elizabeth A., 14
MacIntyre, Alasdair, 131
Medina, Javier, 119
Milo, Daniel S., 129
Miller, Darrow L., 129
Moltmann, Jürgen, 104, 126, 155, 159
Montaigne, Michel, 46
Mortari, Luigina, 160
Mounk, Yascha, 65, 66
Mouffe, Chantal, 94, 97
Musil, Robert, 145

Natoli, Salvatore, 131
Ngomane, Mungi, 153
Nietzsche, Friedrich, 10, 110
Nussbaum, Martha, 129, 131, 154, 157

Oz, Amos, 48, 107

Paul VI, 105
Paz, Octavio, 10, 11, 12
Pannenberg, Wolfarht, 49
Pellegrino, Gianfranco, 133
Perdue, Leo G., 119, 126
Pius XI, 105
Piketty, Thomas, 92
Prigogine, Ilya, 42
Pulcini, Elena, 23, 128

Ramelli, Illaria L.E., 116
Ravasi, Gianfranco, 4, 118
Rafele, Antonio, 23
Ratzinger, Joseph, 78
Recalcati, Massimo, 9, 56
Ribeyro, Julio R., 12, 137
Rice, Richard, 28
Ricoeur, Paul, 43, 156
Rivera, Mayra, 35
Robinson, James A., 66, 88, 89
Rodotà, Stefano, 124
Rosa, Hartmut, 15, 26, 82, 153
Rovelli, Carlo, 82
Roy, Olivier, 27, 113

Author Index

Said, Edward W., 13
Schleiermacher, Friedrich, 28
Schmit, Gerard, 101
Scholem, Gershom, 126
Schopenhauer, Arthur, 53
Scott, Jordan, 9
Sesboüé, Bernard, 159
Simone, Anna, 84
Simmel, George, 23, 24
Sloterdijk, Peter, 81, 82, 110
Smith Adan, 130
Solon, Pablo, 119
Spengler, Oswald, 143
Spinoza, Benedict, 56, 57
Spivak, Gayatri Chakravorty, 29, 44
Studebaker, Steven M., 158

Taylor, Charles, 21, 23, 27, 59, 74, 76, 148
Tonstad, Linn Marie, 62
Tönnies, Ferdinand, 37
Trias, Eugenio, 146

Vasari, Giorgio, 115
Vahanian, Gabriel, 150
Vantini Lucia, 158
Von Balthasar, Hans Urs, 13
Von Rad, Gerhard 119

Waldenfels, Bernhard, 114, 115, 155
Walker-Jones, Arthur, 124, 127, 129
Weber, Max, 11, 22, 48, 95, 113
Weber, Andreas, 120
Westermann, Claus, 125
White, Ellen G., 60, 95, 96, 97, 98, 99, 109

Yao, Joanne, 29

Zambrano, Maria, 158
Zaoui, Pierre, 112
Zehou, Li, 50
Zoja, Luigi, 25, 150

www.ingramcontent.com/pod-product-compliance
Lightning Source LLC
Chambersburg PA
CBHW062043220426
43662CB00010B/1634